D1288023

ADVANCES IN CONTEMPORARY EDUCATIONAL THOUGHT SERIES
Jonas F. Soltis, EDITOR

J. RURY

A
Natural History
of
Place in Education

DAVID HUTCHISON

foreword by
David W. Orr

Teachers College
Columbia University
New York and London

Published by Teachers College Press, 1234 Amsterdam Avenue, New York, NY 10027

Copyright © 2004 by Teachers College, Columbia University

All rights reserved. No part of this publication may be reproduced or transmitted in any form or by any means, electronic or mechanical, including photocopy, or any information storage and retrieval system, without permission from the publisher.

Credits:

The author gratefully acknowledges permission to reprint in Chapter 4 material originally published in the journal *Encounter*, *16*(4). Available on-line: http://www.great-ideas.org.

All chapter photographs by the author.

Library of Congress Cataloging-in-Publication Data

Hutchison, David (David L.)
    A natural history of place in education / David Hutchison ; foreword by David W. Orr.
        p. cm. — (Advances in contemporary educational thought series)
    Includes bibliographical references and index.
    ISBN 0-8077-4470-0 (cloth : alk. paper) — ISBN 0-8077-4469-7 (pbk. : alk. paper)
    1. Place-based education. 2. Place (Philosophy) 3. School environment.
I. Title. II. Series.

LC239.H88 2004
370.11'5—dc22   2004041244

ISBN 0-8077-4469-7 (paper)
ISBN 0-8077-4470-0 (cloth)

Printed on acid-free paper

Manufactured in the United States of America

11 10 09 08 07 06 05 04   8 7 6 5 4 3 2 1

CONTENTS

SERIES FOREWORD

David Hutchison brings a wealth of research and reflection to his highly readable and personal explication of the concept of place in education. As educators, we think, write, and talk a lot about what to teach and how students learn, but we seldom pay much attention to where teaching and learning take place. Yes, we know it happens in schools, in classrooms, labs, and even in auditoriums, study halls, and gymnasiums. But more often than not, these places are invisible backdrops, taken for granted locations that are constructed as neutral spaces we fill in with our educational activities. In this book, David Hutchison helps us to see more clearly the importance of place in education.

Place, for Hutchison, is a multidimensional concept. In its most rudimentary form, it is an individual's perception of and feeling toward a part of his or her world. The saying "There's no place like home" captures this sense of a person's emotional ties to place. We fondly remember places in our past such as homes, churches, streets, playgrounds, fields, streams, and woods. Of course, we also remember negative places like Mrs. Smith's cold and hostile third-grade classroom or the dentist's office. Our emotional reactions to place are crucial in determining how we act in such places. When educators attend to this dimension of place, they can more clearly see what might be needed to make the place of education a more congenial one for students.

Then, too, there is the pedagogical and ideological dimension of educational places. For example, a school or classroom that is consciously designed to underwrite a philosophy of education that believes children should be active learners, collaborating with fellow students in their learning, will look and feel quite different from one designed to place the teacher in authority as the transmitter of subject matter. Hutchison looks at place with regard to such pedagogical and ideological stances as disciplinary initiation, citizenship education, inquiry learning, developmental congruency, community study, and global education.

We also talk and think of place as the proper place of something in relation to other things. Thus, we think and talk about the place of education in a democratic society or in a technological/global economy or in a changing world. To talk of the proper aims of education in society is to talk about the place of education in the larger scheme of things. This sets the direction for educating children and largely determines what will be learned in our schools and how they will be built and furnished.

Using this broad understanding of place, Hutchison nicely weaves the historical with the contemporary. He discusses Pestalozzi, Froebel, Montessori, Waldorf, and open education. He sketches the impact of several 20th-century movements, events and ideas including social reconstructionism, the launching of Sputnik, human capital theory, the *Nation at Risk* report, and school choice. He also deals with school architecture, classroom design, and the current challenge of renewing the infrastructure of American schools. One of his most important contributions is his discussion of cyberspace as a virtual educational place and the challenge it presents to us now and for the future. He also raises crucial questions about the public place of education in society.

This is a book that provides a new perspective on many historical and contemporary taken-for-granted ideas, and as such it is a worthy addition to the Teachers College Press series, *Advances in Contemporary Educational Thought*.

JONAS F. SOLTIS
SERIES EDITOR

FOREWORD

Modern humans are rapidly losing a sense of place, by which I mean the competent and knowledgeable affection for a specific locality. Among other things, the transition to a thoroughgoing modernity has not only forcibly displaced many, but has rendered many more deplaced, without any concept of place or knowledge of why it is important. No longer are we dependent on local agriculture, local energy sources, locally derived medicines, or local places as the context for education. We have become, as ecologist Raymond Dasmann once noted, "biosphere people," provisioned by complex and vast global systems that we cannot comprehend or control. The land around us is increasingly homogenized, becoming everywhere and nowhere places. Strip malls, highways, and commercial establishments look the same whether they are in Phoenix or Philadelphia. The downtown buildings of Tokyo are like those of Los Angeles and Berlin. Our mental landscapes, too, are increasingly homogenized. We are people whose thoughts are increasingly shaped by television; the Internet; urban sprawl; and a homogenized, standardized curriculum for schools. We are often clueless about what we have lost or why.

And what have we lost? Simone Weil once described the need for roots and place as the most fundamental of human needs. I believe this to be true. We are not well equipped to live in a totally abstract world, a "virtual world," as this book notes. Something in us comes undone as our moorings to tangible places, history, and natural history are severed. The story is now old and familiar. The siren call of modernity first creates contempt for tradition, culture, community, and lived places and then the young flee to where life is believed to be exciting and the people are rich. Rural places, whether in Kansas or China, are increasingly impoverished, becoming colonies in the globally extractive economy that mines minerals, soils, fuels, and the souls of people. Urban places, including many city schools, have become traffic-clogged commercial or industrial real estate in the continual undermining of the civic and civilized.

Around the world, there is a counter movement of people who have come to realize that some of the promises of a deplaced modernity are merely hype. And this movement is gaining steam. It has many names and its members march under many different banners, such as historic preservation, slow food, green cities, sustainable agriculture, smart growth, sustainable forestry, indigenous rights, bio-regionalism, eco-villages, non-violence, community renewal, and renewable energy. Whatever their differences, such people understand the need for improved quality (as opposed to increased quantity) of economic activity while maintaining strong local communities, decent neighborhoods, true democracy, prosperous farms, and a natural capital of soils, forests, wildlife, and local traditions. They understand the connections between health, wholeness, and the holy and the deep need to "find [their] place and dig in," as the poet Gary Snyder once put it. They are homecomers.

They also recognize the big numbers of our time for what they are. We are approaching the end of the fossil fuel–powered world. Sometime in the next few years, half of the available oil on earth will have been burned and we will start down the backside of the slope as once described by geologist M. King Hubbert. Even if portable fossil fuels were abundant, we know now that we cannot burn carbonaceous fuels with ecological impunity. Human-driven climatic change is now the wild card in our future. The end of the cheap fossil fuel age will result in changes in virtually everything that we now take for granted, including cheap food, easy mobility, instant gratification, and our ability to offload our ecological and social costs onto others in different places and times. It can, if we are wise enough, mean the end of wars over oil and politics polluted by money. A world powered by sunlight can be, again if we are wise enough, a better world.

In Irish folklore the salmon is regarded as the wisest of species because it knows how to find its way home. We moderns have not yet proven to be as wise. We will need help, beginning with the kind of education that fosters the skills, aptitudes, and wherewithal to live well in specific places. As alert observers of contemporary education know, this is not the direction in which we are heading. Education has been whittled down to a more prosaic and technical thing unrelated to the specifics of place, ecology, and a situated personhood. There are those who intend it to be a source of conformity and thereby a source of comfort to the prevailing powers. In their view, education ought to equip the young for employment in that great scam called the global economy. There is a better vision for education and the life of the mind that is rooted in place. The starting point is a thorough understanding of a natural history of place in education and a clearheaded sense of the reciprocal and intimate relationship between head, hands, heart, and place.

DAVID W. ORR

ACKNOWLEDGMENTS

I am indebted to many people who played key roles in supporting the writing of this book. I am grateful to Professor David W. Orr and Series Editor Professor Jonas F. Soltis, both of whom kindly contributed forewords. Brian Ellerbeck, Eugenia Kopsis, and Aureliano Vázquez Jr. skillfully handled the book at the publisher's end.

I would also like to thank Professor David Booth, who advised me on early drafts of the writing. Professors Gary Knowles, Edmund O'Sullivan, and David Selby also reviewed early drafts of selected chapters. It has been a great privilege to study with Edmund O'Sullivan and David Selby for several years and to teach alongside David Booth at the University of Toronto. Finally, I would like to thank my colleagues at Brock University, with whom I have had the privilege of teaching over the last several years. In particular, I wish to thank Professors John Novak and Adele Thomas, as well as Andrew Short, who provided feedback on selected chapters.

The introductory chapter addresses the importance of my secondary school years in contributing to my early understandings of place in education. I would like to acknowledge the early mentorship of Jim Baker of the School of Experiential Education in Toronto who encouraged me to reflect on my schooling and early work experiences with children in a thoughtful way.

A book about place is enriched through the inclusion of photographs. Most of the photos in this book were taken in the Niagara region where I live. I debated including photographs from multiple school districts across several states. In the end, I believe the choice to focus on a single catchment area nicely underscores an understated theme of this book, namely that *every* school district has hidden within its boundaries a natural history of place in education. We need only choose to look at schools, classrooms, and pedagogy through the lens of place to discover a new way of seeing education. In this regard, I would like to thank Doug Durant and Howard Slepkov of the District School Board of Niagara for helping me to arrange the photo shoots.

Finally, I would like to thank my parents, and sister Sara-Lynn, who have been a constant source of support and encouragement throughout the writing process.

A
Natural History
of
Place in Education

Introduction

PLACE, PEDAGOGY, AND PERSONHOOD

Places . . . define space, giving it a geometric personality. . . . Places are
centers of value. They attract or repel in finely shaded degrees. To attend to
them even momentarily is to acknowledge their reality and value.
—Yi-Fu Tuan (1977, pp. 17–18)

This book explores the intersection of place and education. The topic of place has generally been backgrounded in the study of education, yet the concept of place is integral to a full understanding of the changing land-scape of the K–12 school experience. The chapters that follow discuss the philosophy of place in education and everyday life, competing pedagogies of place, the history of and current trends in school design, the school infrastructure crisis, the relationship between the philosophy of education and classroom design, the move from "real" to "virtual" places in computer-mediated schooling, and the changing public versus market-driven land-scape of education in the United States. The book argues, in part, that pressures on schools associated with declining budgets, competing ideolo-gies, and economic/technological shifts have the potential to radically alter the way in which educational places are constructed and conceived. A discussion of strategies for mediating these pressures and strengthening a sense of place in education concludes the book.

A PLACE TO INSPIRE

The original impulse to write on the topic of place in education occurred to me during the winter of 1985, my next to last year of high school. I was looking forward to university and the promise of pursuing academic stud-ies of my own choice and I already had a good sense of just what those studies would be, at least in a general way. I wanted to be a philosopher of education and it was with this goal in mind that I began reading, on a

cold, wintry night by the fireplace, M. R. Heafford's (1967) biography of
the "Father of Progressive Education," Jean Heinrich Pestalozzi. I had already devoured John Dewey's *Experience and Education*, having chosen it
over the more challenging and (then) inaccessible *Democracy and Education*. In tracing the roots of progressive thought, I was ready to move on to
explore some of the foundational writers of progressive education, most
notably, Rousseau, Pestalozzi, and Froebel. A good place to start would be
with the biographies of these early progressives which, particularly in the
case of the latter two reformers, linked their respective theoretical ideas
to educational practice.

Several things struck me about Pestalozzi's life and work and together
these points helped to frame, in my mind at least, the notion of schools—
and K–12 education more generally—as special places and testing grounds
for innovative and challenging ideas. First, I was surprised to learn that
Pestalozzi's most notable experiments in education at Burgdorf (1800–
1804) and Yverdun (1805–1825) in Switzerland were constantly under
threat of closure, mostly due to financial challenges related to Pestalozzi's
inexperience as an administrator. Pestalozzi began his work with children—
impoverished children no less—fairly late in life, but despite the high praise
and notoriety his schools achieved, he never developed the organizational
and fiscal management skills needed to ensure the long-term stability of
his efforts. Thus, the stress of impending school closure preyed deeply on
Pestalozzi. To this day, this image of Pestalozzi as an embattled reformer
serves as a needed reminder of the precarious nature of educational reform. It is also an image that I carry with me whenever I face challenges
and disappointments in my own teaching.

I also had a second, more pronounced response to the places described
in Pestalozzi's biography. Manifested throughout Heafford's account is the
optimism of an age that was just now awakening to the promise and potential of childhood education. Pestalozzi's work attracted the attention
of European leaders, including royalty, and Pestalozzi himself played host
to numerous dignitaries who visited his schools. There seemed to be,
throughout Europe during the early 1800s, a genuine interest in experimental and innovative approaches to child education, even at high levels
of national governments. Pestalozzi's disciples and other educational reformers were similarly influenced by his thinking. They brought his ideas
home and began implementing them in their own experimental schools
across Europe. In a historic turn of events, one such reformer, a young
German student-teacher, sat at the back of Pestalozzi's class for several
weeks, carefully observing the practice of the master teacher. Soon to
be one of leading reformers of the next generation of educational
progressives, Friedrich Froebel would embrace and then later extend

Pestalozzi's method, inventing the kindergarten along the way. In my book *Growing Up Green*, I traced the legacy of educational reform from Pestalozzi to Froebel and on to progressive and holistic education:

> Through lessons in map and model-making . . . Pestalozzi pioneered the study of place in childhood by having his students explore the terrain and topography of local ecosystems. However, it was left up to one of Pestalozzi's most respected student-teachers to consolidate the child/nature relationship in an even more integral manner. As Pestalozzi's most influential protégé, German-born educator Friedrich Froebel further developed the relationship between the child and nature as established by Pestalozzi and Rousseau and introduced into this mix an even more profound third dimension which embraced a threefold relatedness between humanity, nature, and spirit (God). Froebel is perhaps best known as the founder of the kindergarten. Progressive education appropriated this aspect of his pedagogy, but dismissed those elements of his work which extended from the spiritual realm and potentially threatened a secular view of education. Holistic education, on the other hand, embraced Froebel's conception of the spirit and further developed it as the basis for a new vision of child development and education. (Hutchison 1998, pp. 84–85)

Their philosophical and curricular contributions notwithstanding, it was the spirit of place that characterized the experimental schools of Pestalozzi, Froebel, and other early reformers. This captured my attention. As a young adult reading about the optimism of the age of early progressive education, I was struck by the seemingly coherent fusion of spirit, assuredness, freedom, and educational innovation which seemed to characterize the experimental reform projects of the time. In Pestalozzi's day, there was no such thing as a school district or Department of Education with oversight responsibilities for schools. Pestalozzi and other educational reformers, such as Robert Owen, founded their experimental schools in small villages across Europe and invited local children to attend them, often free of charge. The intersection of an experimental temperament, a romantic philosophy, and unbridled optimism marked the beginnings of the progressive revolution in education from which many educational reformers have never looked back.

A PLACE TO LEARN

Around the time I was reading about Pestalozzi and other reformers, I was also causing a mild degree of grief for my teachers. For example, I can remember standing up during a 12th-grade math class and announcing that "we go to school to learn how not to learn." Although I was an average student, with no discipline problems to speak of, I was disenchanted during most of my high school years. I privately formulated a critique of my schooling, which led me to believe that I was not getting what I needed in a traditional secondary school program. So in grade 13, I transferred to a public alternative school, the School of Experiential Education (SEE) in Toronto. I thrived in this alternative program, improved my marks, and soon began to put my educational musings into writing in a thoughtful way.

As the name suggests, the SEE program is built on the idea that individual and shared experiences should drive learning. New and revisited experiences are both the source and outcome of reflected-upon learning. Learning is contextual, personal, and shared. In conceptualizing this view, the school's curriculum closely follows David Kolb's (1984) experiential learning model, which comprises the stages of concrete experience, reflective observation, abstract conceptualization, and active experimentation. By challenging me to draw from my experiences, on both individual and shared group levels, the SEE program set me on the path of articulating an educational philosophy, which was gleaned in part from my own experience of school and my early work experiences with children.

Until I attended the SEE school, my notion of place in education did not extend beyond the four walls of the classroom. Education was what happened inside these four walls. Life was what occurred outside of the school. Yet the SEE program changed this perception by honoring those learning experiences that occurred outside of the school. (This was an admittedly risky move on the part of the program. Not all students were inclined to "work on themselves" throughout the year and some laxed off.) My teachers encouraged me to reflect on and work through those personal experiences that preceded my entry into the SEE program, particularly my work experience as a summer camp counselor. Such reflections were complemented by overnight trips, first to a small village where our class conducted a community study, and later to an outdoor education center where we explored the stages of group development. In contrast to many traditional class trips, these overnight stays were not separate from or mere add-ons to the instructional program; rather, they were the culmination of a study of group dynamics (in the case of the latter excursion) or the impetus for new learning (in the case of the former). The impact of these excursions on my emerging philosophy of education was to implant in my mind the notion that schools—as places where children go to learn—serve as arbitrary choices for formal education. The existence of schools need not be a given. Throughout the coming years, this notion of flexibility in learning places would frame much of my thinking about education as I studied free schooling, deschooling and, beginning in the 1990s, cyberschooling proposals.

A PLACE TO PRACTICE

During my final year of high school, I was hard at work developing the fundamentals of a philosophy of education and improving my practice as a recreational worker with children. Critical of the perceived authoritarian and irrelevant nature of my own traditional education, I became entranced with the notion of freedom in education—the idea that the individual student is best able to direct one's own learning. In my educational writings, I began to challenge the need for grades, external rewards, and teacher authority. I argued that each student should be granted the freedom to direct his or her own learning according to one's personal aspirations and needs.

To support this educational ideal, I needed an ideal educational place that could serve as a role model for my own work with children. Like many other supporters of free schooling, I found such a place in Summerhill School in England. Founded as a residential coeducational private school by A. S. Neill early in the 20th century, Summerhill served as a testing ground for libertarian principles. The school gained worldwide notoriety with the publication of Neill's 1960 book, *Summerhill: A Radical Approach to Child-rearing*.

Many of my early writings, during my last year of high school and throughout university, focused on Neill's work. One high school paper served as an overview and critique of the Summerhill philosophy. A lengthy first-year university paper traced the development of Neill's libertarian ideals before Summerhill. Yet I was not content simply to revere Summerhill as an ideal educational place in my academic life. I also wanted to put my libertarian ideals into practice in a place where I could personally test my emerging philosophy of education. I found such an opportunity as a summer camp counselor working with children with medical handicaps in a residential camp in northern Ontario. Intent on making the most of my libertarian experiment at camp, I kept a record of my experiences and turned my reflections into a paper upon entry into the SEE school that fall.

The paper that I wrote—aptly titled "The Dismantling of Freedom"—attempted to articulate why I fell so short of my goal of successfully facilitating a camper group following the principles of freedom. By analyzing several discipline incidents, I attempted to articulate how my libertarian principles were almost daily challenged by my camper group's need for structure and guidance. I wrote about the challenge of facing continuing disappointments and setbacks and the need to come to grips with the threatened disintegration of my camper group.

In reflecting on this early focus on freedom, I wonder now if a radical free schooling agenda for education has not represented, throughout most of the 20th century, a shared ideal for many young reformers. (In our increasingly corporate culture, this ideal may well be less attractive now than it was previously.) I know that I have "matured" in my view of free schooling to the point where I now recognize the important role played by adult authority in children's lives. In the years since my freedom experiment at camp, I have proposed and implemented camper programs that use a group dynamics approach to leadership. In these programs, children participate as equals, albeit under the careful guidance of adults, in program planning and problem-solving sessions aimed at addressing discipline situations. Indeed, in *Growing Up Green,* I chronicle such an adult-facilitated approach to working with groups. I also dedicate several pages to a critique of the libertarian vision of schooling and explicitly argue for an authoritative role for parents, teachers, and other caregivers in the lives of children.

IDEALIZED PLACES

Pestalozzi's schools, the SEE school, Summerhill, and summer camp have all, at one time or another, represented an idealized educational place in my mind. During my last years of high school, the optimism and experimental temperament of Pestalozzi's cohorts excited me about the possibilities of educational reform. If I could go back in time to a single moment in educational history, Froebel's visit to Pestalozzi's school in Yverdun might very well be my destination. Or would my destination be Summerhill instead? During my undergraduate years, I was captivated by Summerhill and, for a time, I even debated a visit to Leiston, Suffolk, where the school still operated under the direction of Neill's daughter.

Yet such a visit was not to be. The challenges I faced implementing a libertarian approach as a camp counselor and a growing awareness of the global challenges facing the world led me away from the individualistic impulses of the libertarian philosophy and toward a more holistic, ecological and, indeed, teacher-directed philosophy of education. So, too, my focus on place in education slowly shifted from a fixation on ideal educational places—each characteristically removed from the influence of the surrounding society—to a concern for the vitality of local communities and the wider global environment. I retained my early interest in child psychology, but framed my theory of child development within a constructivist/ holistic framework that emphasized the importance of story, form, earth literacy, and place study as strategies for helping children to develop a functional cosmology of the world, a working theory of how the world works.

This book marks a return to a focus on place, not solely as a curricular area of study, as articulated in *Growing Up Green*, but also as a designated, (usually) physical locale where formal education is deemed to occur. Just as the educational places that were dear to me in my formative years informed my developing educational philosophy, so too the process of writing this book has further clarified my own thinking about special places in education. In the chapters that follow, my interest in the philosophy of education and child development continues to find expression as I explore the relationship of place to educational ideology, school and classroom design, and cyberschooling reform.

Although by no means exhaustive in scope, this book does aim to take a wide, cross-sectional view of the concept of place in education. In general, I have chosen topics that provide the backing for arguments laid out in the concluding chapter. My foremost hope is that this book will inspire readers to forge for themselves meaningful connections between place and education not fully addressed in the text—connections such as the relationship of place to the history of school segregation, sociological critiques of contested places in schools, environmental quality as a predictor of school success, overcrowding in schools, and personalized accounts of schools as remembered places in adulthood. These and no doubt many other educational topics are ripe for in-depth explorations from the perspective of place. Such connections further underscore the importance of the concept of place as a vantage point for studying schools and education, both in the here and now and in the future.

Chapter 1

THE MEANING OF PLACE
IN EDUCATION

*One of the demands that we make of places is that we be able to recognize
them. . . . Built places of real distinction require effort; an effort in the making
and a corresponding effort of recognition. They respond to our queries
because they embody careful, particular thoughts. They may bear the traces
of many imaginings, the scars of conflicting territorial claims. . . . We must
seek the stories in them, piecing together the evidence of our senses
and joining in the action.*
—Donlyn Lyndon (1986, p. 2)

There is a beautiful moment during the graduation ceremony in certain
Waldorf schools that sees each child of the youngest class lead hand-in-
hand into the auditorium a member of the graduating class of the school.
Each graduating 17-year-old, having dedicated nearly a decade and a half
of one's life to the school, is ceremoniously led single file into the auditorium by a 4-year-old child who is just now embarking on a similar jour-
ney. This rite of passage, which is repeated year after year, is first and
foremost a ritual that celebrates the accomplishments of each member of
the graduating class, but it also serves as a temporal marking off of the
significance of "this place called school." For all those who attend the ceremony, this moment is a cherished reminder of the sanctity of this place,
its significance, purpose, and legacy.

Schools are places that are imbued with meaning—both shared and
private. They act as conduits of ideas and practices within which cultural
knowledge, norms, values, attitudes, and skills are passed from one generation to the next. As students, teachers, parents, and citizens, we invest
schools with the responsibility for continually renewing (or perhaps transforming) the social fabric of society. For adults, schools hold the promise
of a secure future life for our children. For students, schools also serve as
formative sites where social roles and moral codes of conduct can be tested
out and practiced. To study the role of place in education is to study the

institutional bridge that ensures our cultural continuance, that connects one adult generation to the next.

An exploration of the role of place in education would be warranted at any time, but the reforms to education that are presently being proposed and implemented surely make this investigation a timely one—one that is perhaps even overdue. This book is written during a period when schools, in wealthy countries all over the world, are facing financial hardships and social pressures that have prompted school districts to search for increasingly efficient and innovative ways to serve students through revamped curricula, private sector cofunding partnerships, high-tech reform, repurposed school facilities, austerity measures, and other strategies. So, too, we are currently in the midst of a technological revolution related to advances in high technology and telecommunications that is presently transforming our notions of work, leisure, and education. It is now old news to say that we are rapidly moving from an industrial-based economy into an information-based society. To succeed within such a society, most workers will need to demonstrate advanced technical, critical thinking, and collaborative skills and quickly adjust to rapid technological and occupational change. In the eyes of those who invest education with the goal of training a skilled workforce, our schools must play an important role in preparing future generations for these new realities by revamping the role of education in society and adjusting accordingly the types of services that schools provide.

The technological shifts that are occurring just now are already altering our notions of place, community, and selfhood. Contemporary notions of place which for centuries have been grounded in the physical experience of neighborhoods and local communities now face serious challenges as networks of individuals linked by global telecommunications replace face-to-face meetings between people and as virtual places in the digital world of Web sites and the Internet replace firsthand contact with people and places in the real world of local communities. The lasting impact of such a fundamental shift in our lifestyles and notions of community and selfhood is yet to be worked out. However, it seems clear that such a fundamental reworking of place will continue to have far-reaching consequences the world over. The fact that public education is now being called upon to actively contribute to this change process begs the need for further investigation. This book argues that the study of place in education can serve as an important vantage point from which to explore many of the changes to education that we are presently experiencing and are likely to experience in the coming decades. By exploring how the notion of place has contextualized educational reform throughout the 20th and early 21st centuries, the chapters that follow articulate a natural history of place in education that aims to serve as a helpful context for exploring educational change in the future.

Can educational reform movements be understood in terms of how they transform the geographical and ideological landscapes of schools and classrooms? What can the study of place in education tell us about the future of educational reform in an age of technological innovation? How might our experience of place in education change in the coming decades? How are ideological battles over the future of schools rooted in competing conceptions of the place of education in society? Is the sanctity of place in education presently under threat? These are some of the critical questions that are addressed throughout this book.

THE MEANING OF PLACE

The term "place" conjures up visions of locality, spatial representations of those places with which we are familiar, and those places the unfamiliarity of which intrigues us. We reside in places, go to work and recreate in places, travel daily through places that are sometimes meaningful to us and other times ignored or taken for granted. We identify with those places that played some formative (if still elusive) role in our childhood years, those places that are associated with good times or bad. The term "place" is imbued with emotion, defined by the boundaries it imposes on space, and informed by the utility to which space is put in our lives. Place can be understood as an individually constructed reality—a reality informed by the unique experiences, histories, motives, and goals that each of us brings to the spaces with which we identify.

Yet place can also be understood as a socially constructed reality. The boundaries that define spaces and the utility to which spaces are put are often shared and understood by a community of people. Even our emotional connections to places (e.g., to home, school, church, or summer camp) have communal origins that are integral to a full understanding of "this place." The significance of place is often enhanced by the personalities and idiosyncrasies of the individuals who populate a place but, as any returning member of a graduating class will tell you, the significance of a place may well endure after our departure. The spirit of place is carried on, if often transformed, by those who come after us.

In addition to its more common usage, the concept of place also has deep philosophical roots. In ancient Greece, Aristotle used the term *topos* to refer to feelings of belongingness that are evoked by the "where" dimension of a person's relationship to the physical environment. Centuries later, Roman philosophers introduced the notion of the *genius loci* or the *spirit of place*, a phrase that has helped to frame much of the academic discussion of place in recent decades. Recent years have also seen a renewed interest in the concept of place as a way of expressing the emotive relationship of person to environment in a variety of disciplines, most notably architecture (Norberg-Schulz, 2000), geography (DeBlij, 2002), psychology (Groat, 1995), environmental philosophy (Orr, 2002), and urban planning (Archibugi, 1997). Yet, despite this renewed attention, the concept of place has continued to remain elusive and contested, well outside the purview of most disciplines and professions. Jonathan D. Sime (1995) underscores this assessment of place and warns of a potentially uncertain research path ahead:

> The concept of place is reaching the early stages of academic maturity. Undoubtedly, there are confusions in the way the concept is used at present. What one wants to avoid is the concept becoming a catch-all "wastepaper basket," a receptacle for a whole range of research and design issues which would otherwise be discarded by whichever subject area is espousing the concept. (p. 28)

Perhaps the most succinct definition of place is given by Christian Norberg-Shulz (1980, p. 18), who defines place as "space plus character." This phrase captures the semiotic and emotional connection of person to space, which gives a place its unique identity. Instead of "designing spaces," place-conscious architects are in the habit of "creating places." They create places that are culturally meaningful and emotionally resonate. To focus on place as space plus character is to balance the geographer's overattention to physical settings with the psychologist's overattention to mind. The discussion below briefly expands on this basic definition of place by situating place research within the context of three of its major disciplinary advocates: phenomenology, human geography, and critical sociology. I have chosen these disciplines in order to give voice to three divergent root metaphors and the way place is constructed within each of them.

The Phenomenology of Place

> [Consider] the experience of fire. Before I ever heard any explanation about the phenomenon of combustion, I had already experienced fire in different situations in my own life. I had experienced its heat, its brightness, and its destructive or purifying character. . . . Phenomenological description aims at retrieving through thought, the original soil of experience, the life world that is assumed by our representations and by scientific knowledge. (Korosec-Serfaty, 1985, p. 68)

The aim of phenomenology is to "return to the things themselves" (Husserl, 1962, p. 8), to return to "that world which precedes knowledge" (Merleau-Ponty, 1967, p. 9). Phenomenologists ask what is the primal, subjective, and precognitive place experience of the human. To be human is to be in a relationship. To know that relationship is to articulate one's sense of spatiality. The primary spatial relationship is that of our orientation to the world. As an ever-present reality, gravity and our erect stature set the vertical dimension of lived experience apart from that of the horizontal landscapes of our existence (Dovey, 1985). From a phenomenological perspective, place is inhabited rather than filled. Out of basic necessity, individuals dwell, find shelter, and arrange spaces for their possessions. They are intentional in their effort to find meaning in settings. Immediate perceptions, memories, anticipations, and hopes all contribute to the historical richness of this experience. Although each individual's experiences are subjective, phenomenologists are engaged in a constant search for the unity (i.e., universality) of meaning in the subjective. This search establishes phenomenology's claim to be a science (Korosec-Serfaty, 1985).

Researchers who apply a phenomenological approach to the study of place in education ask: What is the everyday place experience of teachers and students in school? How are learning spaces implicitly structured to reveal paths and boundaries, private and public spaces? How is the temporal flow of the school day experienced as a mitigating influence on perception? How do children and adults differ in the way that they make sense of a learning space? In what ways is a classroom set apart from or integrated with the school and community that extends beyond its four walls? What can be said of the emotional connection of person to place in education? How are selected learning spaces feared, longed for, or treated ambivalently?

The Geography of Place

> It is possible to visualize a town as consisting only of buildings and physical objects. . . . A strictly objective observer of the activities of people within this physical context would observe their movements much as an entomologist observes [the behavior of] ants. . . . But a person experiencing these buildings and activities sees them as far more than this . . . in short, they are meaningful. . . . The meaning of places may be rooted in the physical setting and objects and activities, but they are not a property of them—rather, they are a property of human intentions and experiences. (Relph, 1976, p. 47)

A focus on meaning, reflection, and theoretical suppositions, rather than immediate, unreflected-upon experience, distinguishes the geographical perspective from the phenomenological tradition. Human geographers explore those factors and influences that bridge the distance between environment, culture, and individual psychological processes (Altman & Chemers, 1980). Place is rooted in how particular places are invested with meaning on both individually and socially constructed levels.

Wayfinding, the process by which people navigate and make their way through a place, emerges as a central theme within this tradition (Perkins, 2001). Places impress themselves upon the human mind which, in turn, constructs cognitive maps to distinguish between five discrete elements of a place: pathways (channels of movement), edges (boundaries between spaces), districts (embedded spaces with individual identities), nodes (concentrated spaces of intense activity), and landmarks (points of reference that provide direction or recognition).

Human geographers ask: What is the nature of the emotional and semiotic relationship of person to environment that is evoked, often in a communal way, by particular settings? How are places constructed, navigated, symbolized, and otherwise conceived? Places are variously judged to be coherent, safe, aesthetic, appropriately scaled, and functional; or alternatively, critiqued for lacking these and other qualities. There is also a clear biocentric line of thought running through this tradition, which laments the loss of natural and aesthetically congruent places throughout the world.

The Sociology of Place

> The physical environment can be understood as a system of three-dimensional, hieroglyphic symbols—a text that conveys information about the social, political, economic, and cultural relations of society. Places not only sustain individuals in a tangible way by providing shelter . . . they [also] tacitly communicate a way of life. (Sutton, 1996, p. xiii)

The aim of critical sociology is to expose the power relations within society that operate in a colonizing fashion to extend patterns of inequity, domination, and subjugation. By deconstructing the physical environment as a visual text—as a structural, rather than topographical narrative—places can be interpreted as cultural sites that are tacitly involved in the production (and reproduction) of social inequities and patterns of domination. Places are judged to be partisan and ideologically charged. They are not value-free or apolitical. The visual texts of places alternatively constrain or empower our potentialities as individuals by restricting access, encompassing various levels of environmental quality, and perpetuating other overt and hidden inequalities. Places shape our consciousness, social identities, behavior, and attitudes. The forces of hegemony and resistance work against each other to reinforce and oppose these processes, respectively.

In education, the critical sociological tradition has found expression through the critical pedagogy movement. In the passage below, Henry A. Giroux, writing in the foreword to Sutton (1996), argues for several of the basic tenets of a critical view of schooling:

> Public schools cannot be seen as either objective or neutral. As institutions actively involved in constructing political subjects and presupposing a vision of the future, they must be dealt with in terms that are simultaneously historical, critical, and transformative. . . . Critical educators need a language that emphasizes how social identities are constructed within unequal relations of power in schools. . . . We [need to] address how schools can become sites for cultural democracy. (p. x)

In taking these pronouncements to heart, critical sociologists, such as Peter McLaren (1989), have focused on particular classrooms, schools, and neighborhoods as the settings for case studies that critique the hegemonic role of education in extending patterns of inequity and domination from one generation to the next. Although a focus on place helps to establish the scope and context for the social drama that unfolds in these studies, the construction of place is rarely in and of itself the sole or primary concern.

A more focused study of school-as-place from a critical sociological perspective can be found in Sharp and Green (1975), who adopt a critical sociological point of view in mapping the discontinuity between educational philosophy and instructional practice in a British child-centered school. (See also Valerie Polakow's [1992] study of early childhood education settings, discussed in Chapter 4.) In 1996, Sharon E. Sutton argued for an environmental text of poverty and privilege in a book that combines narrative accounts of particular school settings with child and author commentaries on the structural foundations that inform such spaces. In her concluding chapter, Sutton asks, "If places are texts that instruct children about a way of life, what types of landscapes might enable them to take leave of their assigned ranks and roles in the hierarchies of the dominant culture?" (p. 197). As with other critical sociological studies, Sutton's research incorporates both descriptive and prescriptive elements that together comprise the social reconstructive agenda of the critical pedagogy movement.

The Study of Home and School

The above perspectives on educational places notwithstanding, it is the study of home that accounts for much of the literature exploring the sense of place in everyday life. Place theorists have applied a number of theoretical understandings to a study of the phenomenological, territorial practices, and temporal qualities of home (e.g., Altman & Werner, 1985). In contrast to this, schools as everyday places which are invested with shared meanings perhaps fall more generally within the purview of social constructivist accounts. Despite its close proximity to child and family life, it is the less place-specific and more institutionally, ideologically, and administratively grounded aspects of school life that tend to get foregrounded. More personal accounts of school life may emphasize the adult-child relational aspects of education (e.g., success stories of teachers working with special needs children), but the significance of particular settings is often ignored or assumed. Although place metaphors such as "setting," "landscape," and "space" are prominently featured in the titles of academic papers, rarely are these words intended to directly refer to the physical settings of schools. Throughout academia and popular culture, where educational places are emphasized, it tends to be specific examples, highly individualized narrative accounts of inner-city challenge and triumph (e.g., movies and television series such as *Teachers*, *The Substitute*, and *Boston Public*), which highlight the emotive relationship of person to place in education. Such place narratives may represent a fertile ground—even a familiar genre—for novels, movies, and popular culture, but they not so subtly reinforce the view that the study of place in education *has no place* except under extraordinary or perilous circumstances. In these and other educational writings, the larger patterns of geography and ideology that connect a broad view of place to the history and philosophy of education tend to remain unacknowledged.

THE MEANING OF PLACE IN EDUCATION

Despite the above caveat, a sense of place has never been very far afield from education. For over a century now, schools have held a special place in the public consciousness. Witness the never-ending public debate over the aims and methodologies of schooling (the focus of Chapter 6). As specialized places dedicated to the education of the young, we invest schools with both shared and contested meanings related to their role in shaping the hearts, minds, and skills of the next generation. Many of us also invest such places with our deepest sentiments and aspirations—for example, the promise of equal opportunity for all, the hopes for a better future life for our children, and the promise of a socially responsible and highly educated citizenry. There is a general recognition, despite competing agendas for reform, that schools should formally inculcate each new generation into the norms and values of society. As formal, (mostly) publicly funded institutions, K–12 schools perhaps remain the last bastion of mandated community involvement in child socialization. As parents and citizens, we count on this bastion to mediate, counter, and offset the unchecked influence of other less formal institutions, such as the peer group, media, and popular culture, by providing a corrective or compensatory measure to our children's education.

Spatiality and Place

Within a single school are a multiplicity of places. Of course, there are classrooms, playgrounds, gymnasiums, auditoriums, music rooms, cafeterias, staff rooms, and myriad other spaces which are formally known by their purpose and function; but place in school is something more than a simple topographic representation of a site. The meanings that students and teachers attribute to such spaces are also important in defining the culture of the school. How we make sense of a space—both individually and collectively—goes a long way in determining how we make use of that space. Our sense of place both empowers and constrains how we approach, utilize, and value the spaces that surround us.

Some places are shared by groups of students, while others are contested. Invisible boundaries separate student cliques on both the elementary school playground and in the high school cafeteria, and in doing so reveal nested places with individual identities and activity patterns all their own. Other nested places have formal functions and scales of activities. Hallways are highly trafficked public spaces, but they are also home to lockers, a student's lone private domain in an otherwise public place. Speaking of private places, some spaces, such as the boys' and girls' locker rooms and restrooms, are little known, but highly speculated upon, by members of the opposite sex. Other places, most notably the detention area, but perhaps also the staff room and principal's office, aim not to be known at all.

In schools, there are clear rules that dictate when to enter and exit a space, where to situate oneself, and how to use a space. Individual classrooms have designated areas that are accessible to all, accessible only with the permission of a teacher, or accessible to the teacher alone. There are large spaces, such as the carpeted areas in early primary classrooms, that are appropriately used for full class lessons and individual desks that are the domain of each student. There are spaces for storing things, completing work, doing "time-outs," and rewarding oneself for work completed.

Temporality and Place

While it is more common to represent place solely in terms of its spatial elements, place is significant not only in the way it gives meaning to the physical makeup of space, but also in the way it structures our temporal use of that space. Our notions of time construct, limit, and otherwise contextualize the meanings that we attribute to places in our everyday lives. In schools, certain times of the academic year, such as the first week of school and the days leading up to exam periods, often seem to move at a faster and more frantic pace than other times. More generally, the temporal rhythm of the school year is structured by opening and closing weeks, summer and winter breaks, exam periods, and culminating activities associated with school plays, competitive sports, graduation, and grade promotion. (For year-round schools, this temporal experience may well be even more complex as groups of teachers and students enter and leave the school at various times.) Researchers have applied selected temporal aspects of place to home environments (Altman & Werner, 1985), but such constructs are also applicable to the temporal flow of the school year.

First, there is the *linear* flow of each school day, with its familiar routine of arrival, opening and closing exercises, class periods, recesses, lunch break, after-school activities, and departure. (The school bell, as a marker of when to enter and exit a space, is a unique but often taken-for-granted fixture of schools. It demands that teachers and students move to their next space at predetermined times, rather than when they are ready to do so. As many teachers know only to well, both the bell and the school's public address system, when used too liberally, have the potential to fracture the flow of ongoing lessons.) Second, there is the *cyclical* flow of each week (or rotary schedule) in which the daily routine is repeated. A cyclical routine establishes the continuity needed by younger children and the individualized time schedules followed by older students. Another cyclical flow marks the transition between seasons, which can have a marked impact on the experience of moving between inner and outer spaces, particularly in the primary grades. Finally, there is the added academic notion of *progressive* time. The passing of each school year serves as a rite of passage that marks off each student's progress through their formal education. The temporal pledge of K–12 education is the promise of a better future life if only one will study hard and "stay in school."

Self-identity and Place

The above paragraphs notwithstanding, place-making in schools is not solely an exercise in the spatial and temporal management of space. School

spirit, pride in sports teams, and a school's competitive standing in relation to other area schools also go a long way in defining a shared and deeply
felt sense of place. On a more personal level, an individual student's sense
of place is intricately related to one's level of self-esteem. In schools, students of differing aptitudes are confronted daily with explicit spaces that
place unique demands on them. As a high school student with an adver-
sity to athletics, for example, I dreaded my occasional visits to the school
gymnasium. In fact, I avoided such visits at all costs. Instead I found so-
lace in the music room where my talents were more fully appreciated. By
the time I graduated from high school, I had visited the gymnasium so
infrequently that I failed to develop a clear picture of what the gymnasium at my school actually looked like. (For a high school so caught up
with athletics this was an outright travesty.) Yet I had an intimate knowledge of the layout and functioning of the school's music room, and even
came to view this space as a sort of safety net, a security blanket from which
to escape from an otherwise intimidating environment.

I suspect that many adolescents have had experiences similar to my
own. After all, gymnasiums *can* be threatening places for students who
lack confidence in their athletic prowess. And yet it occurs to me that most
students and teachers, to varying degrees, will likely develop an attachment to one or more spaces in their school—for example, to a classroom,
the cafeteria, the "smoking corner," the principal's office, or the staff room.
As a high school student, I never once entered the staff room—it was "un-
known" to me and to most other students. A sign on the door made it clear
that this room was off limits to us. Yet the staff room surely impacted on
our teachers' experience of place. Indeed, for some teachers it likely provided the same feeling of security that the music room afforded me.

Developmentalism and Place

The above observations are not limited to the secondary school. In fact,
differences in the ways in which teachers and students make sense of place
may be most pronounced in elementary school where the age discrepancy
is at its greatest. Consider, from the perspective of place, the playground
experience of a young child and her teacher. The teacher is responsible
for supervising the children at recess so he takes a wide view of the playground, watchful of the numerous clusters of children at play. He positions himself at a spot where he can best see a majority of the playground.
As it is a wintry day, he is intensely aware of the cold and perhaps even
keeping an eye on the time. Meanwhile, the young child's attention is
focused on her immediate play environment, perhaps a favorite space
where she plays each recess. She is active and engaged, impervious to the

freezing temperature and the passing of time. Now ask that child and teacher to take you on a tour of the playground. Who provides the most detailed accounting of the space? Who appears to invest the playground with the "most" meaning? The playground is the child's domain, regulated at a macro level by adults but painstakingly managed at a micro level by small clusters of children at play.

THE MEANING OF PLACE IN CHILDHOOD

Differences in the way in which a teacher and child view a playground are related not only to the unique role each plays in a school, but also to differing developmental experiences. As public institutions dedicated to the education of the young, schools are unique in their intergenerational makeup. Children and adults share the same space, and work, learn, and play alongside one other, yet each, to a certain degree, makes sense of the school in different ways. Unlike places in most other social institutions, place in education not only has spatial and temporal roots, but developmental roots as well. To ignore the developmental aspects of place is to fail to address the rich complexity of children's place-making experiences in education.

Understanding how children gradually come to know the world as they mature resides within the domain of child psychology. Place theorists have made important contributions to the study of place perception in childhood by exploring children's construction of play spaces, their maturing understanding of world geography (Wiegand, 1992), and their ability to decipher and design neighborhood maps (Sobel, 1998), among other research agendas. The contributions of place theorists run the gamut from clinical analyses of children's spatial abilities (Sack, 1980) to holistic accounts of children's place-making activities at various stages of development (Hart, 1979). Sadly, however, the results of these investigations have rarely been applied to educational practice. The irony, as will be pointed out in Chapter 4, is that educational reformers nevertheless make philosophical judgments about children's development which then have dramatic implications for the way that classrooms and other educational spaces are organized.

Most developmental psychologists agree that the newborn, insofar as she or he has not yet differentiated oneself from the objects and environments that surround her or him, has no conception of place as distinct from self. Recognizing the limits of one's body, where "I" ends and the rest of the world begins, may well be the first place lesson of childhood. Gradually, through taste and touch, infants come to differentiate themselves from the external world. They begin to attend to the permanence and proximity of objects and the constancy of each object's size and shape. Although a sense of object permanency is well-established by the age of 2, several more years will need to pass before the child has a complex, adult-like understanding of place. Asked to take another's perspective in describing a room that she is in, a child younger than six is apt to represent the room from her own point of view (if she offers any description at all). The ability to take the perspective of another is a basic conceptual skill that confounds the concrete, egocentric, and pictorial sensibilities of the younger child. Yet it is a necessary spatial ability if the child is ever to represent, transform, and otherwise "act on" places, in a three-dimensional way, as it were, in her mind. Only with the maturing faculties of mind, faculties that accompany her growth into and beyond middle childhood, will the child develop the place sensibilities of an adult.

The above paragraph represents the development of place perception as a gradual transition from the immature, preconscious place experience of the unborn child to a more mature place consciousness that matches the cognitive sensibilities of adults. This progressive view of place finds its roots within a classic Piagetian model of cognition. Within such a perspective, changing notions of place are judged to be a function of the maturing cognitive structures of mind. Such structures are both universal (i.e., innate) and individualistic (i.e., internally regulated by the individual child). Although the development of place perception is an active process (i.e., the child "acts" on the world to build up her mind), there is little role for language, the social context, or emotions within such a design. Rather, the child's development of mind, including her maturing understanding of place, is judged to be a purely cognitive, self-regulated, and acultural exercise. Within such a view, the language and symbolic systems of a culture, the uniqueness of particular settings, and the emotional and social lives of children play little if any role in the development of place perception in childhood.

The above cognitive-developmental view of childhood represents the dominant tradition in child psychology. This perspective presents a detailed if somewhat restricted view of child development in which the social context is of little relevance. Quite a contrary perspective is put forward by cultural constructivist researchers who argue for a more holistic view of place perception in childhood, one that takes account of the richness of children's social, emotional, and inner lives and the cultural contexts within which children grow up. Many constructivists argue for an ecological model of place (see Figure 1.1) that highlights various institutional and community influences on child socialization (Matthews, 1992). Other place theorists focus on children's constructivist endeavors in forging a place of their

FIGURE 1.1. The ecology of place in childhood.

own. Edward S. Casey (1997), in his seminal review of the philosophy of place, captures the implicit wonder of a child's first encounters with place from the vantage point of the holistic researcher:

> Lived place thrives—is first felt and recognized—in the differentiated and disruptive corners, the "cuts," of my bodily being-in-the-world. This is why the child's experience of place is so poignantly remembered; in childhood we are plunged willy-nilly into a diverse (and sometimes frightening) array of places. . . . The extraordinary sensitivity of the child's lived body opens onto and takes in a highly expressive place-world that reflects the discriminative and complex character of the particular places that compose this world. (p. 237)

Especially during middle childhood (ages 6 to 12), ritualized play often manifests itself in ganglike activities complete with secret hideaways, clubhouses, and forts. Here the spirit of play and place are bound up together in a unique fantasy world of secrecy, adventure, and challenge. The cross-cultural preoccupation of both boys and girls with secret meeting places, forts, and other "favorite places" (Sobel, 1993)—both "discovered" and built by children—suggests that, like play, place "is structured differently in juvenile life than at later ages; it is much more critically defined. It is intensely concerned with paths and boundaries, with hiding places and other special places for particular things" (Shepard, 1977, p. 8). In middle childhood, such juvenile play space is often configured in its membership to both purposefully include and exclude, to provide "retreat, solitude, and disengagement" for the lucky few.

I suggested earlier that most educational philosophies draw a clear distinction between children's construction of place (which is relegated to play) and their formal learning (the function of school). Nevertheless, there have been a few lone attempts to harness children's need to construct place by turning children's place-making initiatives into quasiformal educational programs. The Adventure Playground movement, which gained prominence during the 1970s, reflects this sentiment (Bengtsson, 1972). The movement was founded on the belief that children should be encouraged literally to construct and take ownership of their play environments—that is, *their* places—using a variety of building materials and tools, including wood, nails, and hammers. To this day, one of my most vivid memories of place in education arose from my role as a project leader supervising children at an Adventure Playground in Toronto. It was the uneasy realization that accompanied my standing on the roof of a two-story building—a building entirely planned and constructed by a group of 8- to 12-year-olds.

THE PHILOSOPHY OF PLACE IN EDUCATION

A developmental perspective of place could, on its own, provide a wealth of material for the study of place in education. As educators, we might well ask ourselves to what degree we take into account the changing place experience of children in formulating educational programs for various grade levels. Indeed, a developmental perspective on place is central to the discussion in later chapters. However, so much of what happens in schools has less to do with our keen observations of children than it does with our ideological commitments to particular ways of teaching. Hence there is a need to acknowledge another important perspective on place in education—namely, a philosophical perspective that addresses the ideological and curricular dimensions of teaching. For it is within such a context that many of the current reform proposals for education are being forwarded. Moreover, as will be argued in later chapters, the impact of these reforms on our conceptions of place in education may well be significant.

Imagine for a moment that you are visiting a particular classroom for the first time (see Figure 1.2). The door to the classroom is slowly opening and the classroom itself is just now coming into view. What is the first thing you tend to notice? I argue that it is the arrangement of the students' desks. Are they arranged into rows or grouped together in clusters of four or five? Do they leave room for a carpeted area or other open meeting space? We deduce a lot from the arrangement of the desks. We tentatively draw conclusions about the educational philosophy of the teacher, the teaching methodology in use, the types of learning experiences that are occurring, the activity level of the students, and perhaps even the performance level

FIGURE 1.2. Our first glimpse of a classroom provides us with important visual clues regarding the educational philosophy of the teacher and the teaching methodologies in use.

of individual students relative to their seating positions. Our glimpse of the layout of a classroom provides us with important visual clues about what life may be like in that class. In reflecting on our observations, we make provisional judgments about the goings-on in the classroom from the standpoint of our own philosophical leanings.

When made overt, an educational philosophy comprises a set of explicit beliefs about the nature of the educational process. In a general sense, an educational philosophy serves as an underlying rationale for the curriculum and methodology of a particular approach to teaching. It provides answers to questions related to the purpose of education, the role of the school in society, and our obligations to future generations. It further makes clear the roles to be fulfilled by teacher and student, indicates what aspects of a student's life are within the pervue of the school or learning situation, and (often subtly) dictates whose values will dominate the educational process itself. Throughout the 20th century, we witnessed the rise and fall of several educational philosophies, each making its mark on education with varying degrees of success. Throughout the last 50 years, the two most dominant philosophies have been the back-to-basic and progressive education movements. Educational commentators often speak of the "swinging of the pendulum" to describe the process by which these two competing ideologies contest gains made by the other and attempt to influence public opinion. The popular media has tended to dichotomize the debate over the fundamental aims of schooling, pitting the merits of the back-to-basic's call for a renewed focus on basic skills against the progressive philosophy's attention to the interests and affective needs of the individual child.

Most surveys of the back-to-basic and progressive philosophies tend to push to the background the role of place in education in favor of a focus on curriculum and teaching methodologies. Yet the notion of place is never very far removed from the underlying suppositions of these two competing agendas for reform. Both philosophies answer a key question that will be asked of a number of reform agendas throughout this book: How should places in education be physically and pedagogically constructed? The varied answers to this question both define and limit the role of education in the eyes of each philosophy and help determine how place is taught (Chapter 2), schools are designed (Chapter 3), and classrooms are organized (Chapter 4).

Chapter 2

A PEDAGOGY OF PLACE

Geography is a discipline in serious trouble. An important cause of some of geography's problems is the relative absence of philosophic inquiry into the nature of the discipline's roles in the educational process. . . . Few analysts have asked: Why should we teach geography? Why has geography been taught the way it has? . . . Into this unquestioning school climate, more and more teachers fresh from teacher education programs enter.
—Joe L. Kincheloe (2001, p. 673)

Several years ago I visited an outdoor education center not very far from where I lived at the time. I witnessed firsthand the environmental activities in which visiting sixth grade students were engaged as they toured the center and rotated between a number of outdoor learning stations. The students began with a tour of the school, which was a model of environmental and energy efficiency. They then completed a number of outdoor activities, each of which introduced an important ecological principle.

At one environmental station the tour guide suddenly stopped the students and began speaking very sternly to them, abruptly quelling the spirited mood of the group. His words were honest, but his tone was intimidating, and it left the students (and me) feeling very uncomfortable. For some time, he ranted on about the serious damage humans are doing to the planet and, in doing so, he expressed very little optimism that the world might ever recover. He placed full responsibility for the environmental crisis on the backs of these 11- and 12-year-old children and their parents. He chided the students for not doing more to save the Earth and, in short, shamed them. I don't know if this leader's diatribe was meant to serve as some sort of environmental "shock therapy" or not, but his approach to the pedagogy of environmental education disturbed me deeply and it left a lasting impression. In fact, it served as the impetus for the "gift of time" principle I would later articulate in my book on environmental education.

There are so many ways to teach children about the environment. Using scare tactics is, of course, one approach, but there are so many others. (Citing the use of scare tactics is very often the first objection raised by those environmental education opponents who would like to see all teaching of environmental values stripped from the curriculum [Hutchison, 2003].) In schools where environmental education is taken seriously, teachers and students conduct pond studies, grow gardens, clean up the local environment, and discuss environmental issues. Although they are no doubt all worthwhile, each of these approaches does amplify a certain way of viewing the environment while dampening others. For example, some environmental education programs (e.g., community gardening) privilege the study of the local over the study of the global. Other environmental strategies (e.g., world study) instead privilege the global by stressing the interconnections between environment, economics, conflict, and development at an international level. There are also environmental education approaches (e.g., acclimatization) that aim to nurture a psychosocial affinity for the natural world, an affective connection that promotes a continuity between self and world (Van Matre, 1974). Other arguably more intellectual strategies instead amplify the critical dimensions of the environmental impasse in terms of moral/philosophical crises in modernity, consumption, and economics (Bowers, 1995).

In stepping back from this environmental vantage point, this chapter explores six competing pedagogies of place more generally and shows how the educational philosophies inherent to each argue for a particular construction of place in K–12 education (see Table 2.1). While the next two chapters focus on the physical construction of educational spaces (i.e., school and classroom design), the philosophies reviewed in this chapter serve to remind us that, when it comes to teaching and learning, educational institutions are as much ideological constructions of place as they are physical buildings.

The six philosophies are: disciplinary initiation, citizenship education, inquiry learning, developmental congruency, community study, and global education. Each sets clear boundaries for what students ought to study on the topic of place. These boundaries are determined in part by debates over:

- *The acquisition of knowledge.* Two of the six philosophies (disciplinary initiation and citizenship education) call on students to acquire an explicit knowledge base that can be communicated as part of a core curriculum. The remaining philosophies view knowledge as a cultural construction which is intricately related to the context of the places under study and/or the lived experience of students.
- *The scale of place.* Four of the six philosophies subscribe to the view that the study of place should focus on a particular scale of place—

TABLE 2.1. Educational philosophy and the pedagogy of place.

	Disciplinary Initiation	Citizenship Education	Inquiry Learning
Root Metaphors	Discipline/ Understanding	Nation/ Patriotism	Child/ Self-development
Aim	To instill in students a solid understanding of the major disciplinary traditions.	To instill in students a solid knowledge of and appreciation for the home country.	To heed the learning styles, aptitudes, and interests of the individual student.
Place Focus	A strong focus on geography and other place-related subdisciplines (e.g., landscape art and natural history). The wisdom, structure, and methodologies of each discipline are emphasized.	A strong focus on national/state geography and the structure of government. Character education is emphasized (e.g., reciting the pledge of allegiance and team sports.)	A strong focus on inquiry, problem-solving, and reflection on experience. Learning activities relate to student interests, experiences, and personal goals. Celebrates a diversity of place contexts.
Knowledge Acquisition	Follows a transmission path. For the uninitiated, knowledge is inculcated. A strong disciplinary focus.	Follows a transmission path. Knowledge is inculcated. A strong societal focus.	Follows a transaction path. Knowledge is actively constructed. Balances an individual / societal focus.
Values	The value of scholarly inquiry is absolute. Intellectual, aesthetic, and moral judgments derived from scholarly inquiry are promoted over subjective values.	Values are absolute. Patriotism and nationalism are promoted. Tradition and individual responsibility to society are emphasized.	Values are relative. Cooperation and social participation are promoted. Individual self-development through reflection on experience and values clarification approaches is emphasized.
Curriculum	A core curriculum that can be explicitly communicated to students. The sovereignty of segregated disciplines is emphasized.	A core curriculum that can be explicitly communicated to students.	A child-centered curriculum that is derived from the aptitudes and interests of the individual student.
Instructional Path	Inculcation of disciplinary knowledge.	Inculcation of national knowledge and values.	Reflection on experience.
Scale of Place	Privileges the study of disciplines over an allegiance to any particular scale of place.	Privileges the study of the nation.	Privileges the aptitudes and interests of the individual student learning in a classroom community. Also privileges diverse place contexts including the esoteric, macro, and micro.

Developmental Congruency	Community Study	Global Education (Critical/Activist)
Child/ Developmental Experience	Neighborhood/ Community Membership	World/ Social Activism
To heed the developmental experience of the individual child.	To nurture in students a solid knowledge of and appreciation for the local community.	To empower students to respond effectively to social and environmental challenges.
A strong focus on each child's developmental experience of place, including home, found spaces, favorite places, pathways, routes, and developing spatial sensibilities.	A strong focus on the natural and built environments of the local community, its innermost workings, cultural artifacts, history, and peoples. School/community partnerships are promoted.	A strong focus on contemporary social issues and current events. Structural inequities between regions are studied. Critical thinking and social action skills are taught and practiced.
Follows a transformation (i.e., developmental) path. Knowledge is actively constructed. A strong individual focus.	May follow a transmission, transaction, or transformation (i.e., social action) path. A strong societal focus.	Follows a transformation path. Knowledge is actively constructed. A strong societal focus.
Values are relative. The congruency of curriculum with a child's developing sense of place is emphasized. Lessons honor the way children see the world.	Values are relative and rooted in the local community context. Social participation and contributions to community development are emphasized.	Values are relative. Critical reflection and social criticism are promoted. Environmentalism, social justice, and civil rights are emphasized.
A developmentally congruent curriculum that is derived from each child's developing sense of place.	A community-centered curriculum that is derived from the local neighborhood context.	A global curriculum that is derived from a comparison of disparate regions of the world.
Congruence with developmental experience.	Immersion into the local community.	Problemitizing of global challenges.
Privileges the developmentally sensitive place experience of the individual child.	Privileges the study of the local community and neighborhood.	Privileges the global, the intersection of local and global, and interconnections/ structural inequities between regions.

nation, neighborhood, or the individual meaning-making experience of the child.

- *Values.* One philosophy (citizenship education) argues that schools should teach a proscribed set of values regarding place. Another (disciplinary initiation) emphasizes scholarly knowledge over the subjective experience of place. Still another (global education) argues that schools should problemitize place at an international level.

Any effort to compartmentalize a set of competing educational agendas invariably leads one to foreground the ideological differences between each and move to the background the ways in which competing philosophies often get diluted and melded into one another in practice. To counter this tendency, this chapter closes by suggesting two pathways by which educators can teach multiple agendas for place study in an integrated way.

DISCIPLINARY INITIATION

Advocates of disciplinary initiation begin with the premise that exemplary schools function primarily as scholarly institutions. Over time, schools consciously induct students into thinking like geographers, historians, scientists, writers, artists, and so on. Supporters argue that curriculum writers can explicitly delineate for teachers a core knowledge base, skill set, and set of aesthetic/moral sensibilities that students should respectively master, become proficient at, and learn to appreciate (Savage & Armstrong, 2004). In terms of place, a student's knowledge base and skill set is likely both defined and limited by the underlying cognitive structures, methodological tools, and subject matter of geography as a unique and valued discipline within academia. The study of natural history, landscape painting, and other place-related subdisciplines might also be undertaken to complement the study of geography.

Disciplinary advocates argue for the worthiness of their philosophy on the basis that the discipline of geography has evolved—tried, tested, and true, so to speak—over several centuries through the pioneering efforts of geographers who, in a thorough and thoughtful way, have collectively built up, challenged, revised, and built up again the underlying cognitive structures and knowledge base of what we now know about the world's physical and human geography. Similarly, the tools and methodologies employed by geographers have been developed and refined over time. In this sense, geography is a tested discipline and, therefore, worthy of in-depth study by students. Similar arguments can be put forward for other subject areas, including literature, history, the sciences, philosophy, and the arts, among others.

Each of these disciplines is seen to address and exercise a unique cognitive, aesthetic, or cultural modality which is judged integral to the human condition. Moreover, each of these modalities explores at its core a root metaphor (e.g., place in the case of geography) which is not reducible to the root metaphor of any other discipline (e.g., time, in the case of history). A well-rounded education inducts students into the underlying structures of key academic disciplines that together form the scientific, aesthetic, and moral foundations of human culture. With regard to place, students gradually learn to see the world from the perspective of the geographer. They receive geographic instruction in class and apply what they have studied to geographic problems in the real world. They learn to intelligently choose the right tools for the job from a geographer's methodological toolset. In short, students begin to think like geographers.

Many advocates of disciplinary initiation tend to shun pedagogical fads and curricular reforms that weaken geography as a distinct and sovereign subject area within schools. In particular, they resist progressive reform efforts to remake the curriculum into thematic (rather than disciplinary) units of study. Thematic and interdisciplinary studies are judged to weaken the integrity of geography and other disciplines and promote a study of place which is at best cursory, shallow, and not grounded on good science (Neatby, 1953; Miller & Seller, 1990).

Many elementary and most secondary school programs subscribe (at least at an administrative level) to something akin to a disciplinary initiation focus, but only as students get older. In the primary and junior grades, history and geography are often taught as a unified thematic area (i.e., social studies), but with the onset of adolescence and the emergence of the critical powers of intellect (*formal operations*, to use Piaget's term), history and geography become split off from one another and are thereafter treated as distinct academic subject areas for the balance of a student's education. At this point, specialist teachers who have studied geography extensively in college are likely to take over a student's place education from generalist teachers. Such a move has important implications for the experience of place in schools, as students begin a rotary program of instruction which takes them from room to room and specialist teacher to specialist teacher throughout the school day.

Of the many advocates for disciplinary initiation, it is perhaps Howard Gardner who is the most familiar to educators. (Elements of Gardner's thought, including his theory of multiple intelligences, also resonate strongly with the inquiry learning philosophy discussed later in this chapter. Other

elements of Gardner's thought serve to problematize the more conservative dimensions of the disciplinary initiation perspective.) In his book, *The
Disciplined Mind*, Gardner writes:

> I call for an education that inculcates in students an understanding of major
> disciplinary ways of thinking . . . Within [these] disciplinary families, it is
> important that students study substantial topics in depth . . . Students should
> probe with sufficient depth *a manageable set of examples* so that they come to
> see how one thinks and acts in the manner of a scientist, a geometer, an
> artist, an historian . . . The purpose of such immersion is *not*—I must stress—
> to make students miniature experts in a given discipline, but to enable them
> to draw on these modes of thinking in coming to understand their world.
> (Gardner, 1999, pp. 117–118)

The above quotation points to an important ideological notion that
goes hand in hand with the disciplinary philosophy. In keeping with the
focus on scholarly knowledge, disciplinary advocates subscribe to a transmission approach to knowledge acquisition as evidenced by Gardner's use
of the word "inculcate" in the first sentence. (Note that this does *not*
imply a transmission approach to teaching and learning. Many disciplinary advocates, including Gardner, call for participatory and dialectical approaches to instruction.) Disciplinary knowledge is valued, the untested
and often misguided mythical sensibilities of the unschooled mind are
only valued insofar as they provide a pathway for working toward disciplinary understanding (Gardner, 1991). Supplanting students' mythical
and wrongheaded assumptions about the world with scientifically tested,
aesthetically valued, and morally reasoned understandings is among the
most laudable goals of education in the eyes of disciplinary advocates.

Within the context of the study of place, there is little support for allowing students to construct, by and for themselves, a personal knowledge base which is not closely tied to or drawn from geography as a tested
and established discipline. Rather, the scope and content of what students
learn about place should reside within the pervue and domain of geography and other place-related disciplines. Each of the activities in which students participate, as well as the real-world place challenges they problem
solve, should aim to deepen their identification with geography as an established mindset that can help them go forward confidently in the world.

Although disciplinary initiation follows a transmission path to knowledge acquisition, the ultimate aim, for many supporters, is to nurture stu-
dent-geographers who are ready to contribute their part, no matter how
modest, to the geographic field of study and, in doing so, grow or even transform our geographical understanding of the world. Hence, a place study
orientation that begins by inducting students into the discipline of geogra-

phy aims, once proficiency has been established, to "free" students so that they can make their own mark on the geographic field, thus contributing to its continued development and our knowledge of the world around us.

CITIZENSHIP EDUCATION

Disciplinary initiation is to scholarship as citizenship education is to nationalism. Both philosophies argue for a transmission approach to knowledge acquisition in that what is learned is largely determined from without. In both cases, students are being initiated (or socialized) into specific ways of thinking. Both philosophies also argue that curriculum writers can explicitly delineate for teachers a core knowledge base that students should master. Where these two ideologies differ is in their contrasting views of the role of values in education, as well as the differing wells of knowledge from which curricular content is to be drawn.

For disciplinary advocates, value judgments, especially those not supported by scholarly, scientific, aesthetic, and/or moral/philosophical reasoning, are to be avoided when studying place and other topics. For example, the study of geography requires an objective aloofness on the part of the student researcher who maintains her neutrality, judiciously employs the tools of the geographer, and only forms judgments on the basis of the preponderance of the evidence. Advocates of citizenship education, on the other hand, argue that elementary and secondary schools are cultural as well as scholarly institutions and, as such, they have a crucial role to play in child socialization, including the teaching of values (Savage & Armstrong, 2004). In sustaining across generations a strong sense of nationhood, schools perform an important service in forging in students a common national identity and in teaching an agreed-upon set of values that underlie what is required for effective citizenship within society. Citizenship education emerges from this cultural vantage point to promote a place study agenda focused squarely on nurturing "good citizens" with strong characters who feel both a sense of pride in their country and have a solid understanding of their country's geography to support and inform that pride.

Place education within a citizenship orientation is very likely to begin early in kindergarten by physically situating the United States or Canada (in this example) both within the world community and within the North American continent (ideally by using a globe). Over the course of the next 6 years, elementary school students in the province of Ontario will be introduced to the physical regions of Canada (physical geography) and the influence of these physical regions on settlement and urbanization patterns (human geography), among other topics (Ontario Ministry of Education and Training, 1998). Students will study Canada's system of governance (federal, provincial, and municipal) and be expected to memorize political boundaries, including the names and locations of Canada's ten provinces and three territories, as well as their capital cities. The further study of Canada's natural and built environments, including the nation's major waterways and transportation links, will also be undertaken, but simply memorizing the names and locations of landmarks will not be sufficient. Rather, steadily nurturing a familiarity with and an appreciation for the nation's natural resources, major industries, exports, multicultural makeup, and other amenities will also be critical. Although the primary focus of a student's attention will be on the home country, other nations will not be ignored altogether; rather, the United States and a few other select countries will be studied *in relation* to Canada. For Ontario students, the study of trade and diplomatic relations, migration patterns, and other connections that bind Canada to other nations will help further situate Canada within the world community without shifting the focus from Canada in any major way.

A focus on learned knowledge marks one-half of the citizenship education philosophy but, as noted above, there is also a more controversial second half to this position which focuses on values and attitudes. As an approach to teaching values, citizenship education has a long history within American education. It was an original mission of the common school to impart to students a core set of American and Judeo-Christian values associated with membership in a liberal democracy and instill in children good character. In this regard, promoting literacy in children was judged to be key, as were strict lessons in morality and behavior, sometimes reinforced through the use of assertive disciplinary techniques. Over the 19th and 20th centuries, advocates of citizenship and character education would gradually adopt something of a more subtle approach to the teaching of values, especially as the separation of church and state became more formalized and advocacy for public schools as secular and multicultural institutions gained favor. Today, the citizenship education philosophy (at least at an explicit level) most widely influences *what* students learn in schools, rather than what they *value*. The enculturating role traditionally played by character education has largely been lost or diluted as many schools aim for value neutrality and guard against challenge from civil rights advocates and parent groups that represent a diversity of religious, cultural, and moral points of view.

Yet, despite this, values *are* taught—both explicitly, as a component of the formal curriculum; and implicitly, as part of the informal curriculum— as teachers discipline students; model appropriate behavior; and variously promote sharing, cooperative learning, team play, and other seemingly innocuous values in their daily interactions with students. Embedded in school routines are other more pronounced nods to the citizenship education philosophy. Each morning students sing the national anthem and recite the pledge of allegiance. So too, citizenship education *within* the school community is nurtured through athletic competitions with other area schools and the promotion of "school spirit." Finally, in the wake of terrorist attacks on U.S. soil, feelings of patriotism are running high in American society, which is surely impacting school programs, including the explicit curriculum, especially in terms of how the place of the United States in the world community is taught to students.

E. D. Hirsch (1987) is perhaps the most well-known advocate for citizenship education. His book, *Cultural Literacy*, closes with a 50-plus page list of the specific content that every culturally literate American should know. In arguing for the citizenship education orientation, Hirsch underscores the importance of tradition and cultural continuance to this philosophy:

> Stability, not change, is the chief characteristic of cultural literacy. Although historical and technical terms may follow the ebb and flow of events, the more stable elements of our national vocabulary, like George Washington, the tooth fairy, the Gettysburg Address, Hamlet, and the Declaration of Independence, have persisted for a long time. The stable elements of the national vocabulary are at the core of cultural literacy and for that reason are the most important contents of schooling. (p. 29)

It is the need to induct students into a common cultural vocabulary, as well as a shared set of cultural sensibilities, which Hirsch and other citizenship educators cite as key to sustaining a strong American democratic society. It follows from this that knowledge is to be acquired by students, rather than independently constructed by them, by and for themselves. As with disciplinary initiation, students may engage in all kinds of interactive, exciting, and rewarding activities in which they appear to be independently constructing the knowledge and values they are learning, but these activities have very likely been purposefully designed to evoke a certain set of responses in students—responses that nurture their citizenship identities and teach a core set of knowledge and values.

INQUIRY LEARNING

In sharp contrast to both disciplinary initiation and citizenship education, advocates of inquiry learning favor the coconstruction of implicit, contextualized knowledge, grounded on individual and shared experience, over an explicit, core curriculum that is predetermined and trans-mitted to students by an external authority (Miller & Seller, 1990). Inquiry learning shares with disciplinary initiation a focus on geography skills, but supporters of inquiry learning see no problem in integrating skill sets across a variety of disciplines and allowing students to develop their own unique skill sets that complement their individual learning styles, aptitudes, and interests. Whereas the advocates of disciplinary initiation take their cue from their subject, inquiry learning proponents take their cue from indi-vidual students, paying particular attention to the lived context of each student's daily life, both in and out of school.

Inquiry learning is rooted in an experiential approach to education (as alluded to in the Introduction) in which a student's learning experi-ences are first reflected upon at a personal or shared level and only then conceptualized within the context of what is already known at an aca-demic level about the topic under study (Kolb, 1984). This process ideally leads students to share what they have learned in creative and personally meaningful ways (e.g., through reflective writing) and ask new questions of the original learning experience, by returning to it, extending it, or entering into a new but related experience with a more advanced set of questions to answer. Thus, an inquiry lesson on place both leads from and into a learning experience which, in turn, "bookends" the teaching and learning process by actively involving students in a study of their world.

It is not by mere chance that inquiry learning is the first orientation to garner such specific methodological attention in this chapter. Whereas advocates of disciplinary initiation and citizenship education are likely to organize the curriculum into carefully sequenced content categories, in-quiry learning proponents instead foreground methodology over content. It is the wide variety of research, problem solving, group work, and many other skills practiced by students over multiple grade levels that are most valued by supporters of inquiry learning. Ideally, as students become in-creasingly proficient in applying such skills to new topics and real-world problems, they will also come to capitalize on and metacognitively view their individual learning styles, aptitudes, and interests as unique expres-sions of who they are as individuals.

Inquiry learning has had something of a wild ride in American edu-cational history. Progressive education, discovery learning, open educa-tion, the new math, and whole language learning all trace their roots back to the inquiry learning philosophy which has seen its influence both rise and fall several times over the 20th century (Miller, 1997). Elements of inquiry learning are to be found in a (perhaps declining) number of ele-mentary school classrooms across the United States, some of which em-ploy thematic, interdisciplinary, or centers-based approaches to teaching social studies, similar to open plan learning (Chapter 4). The success of inquiry learning has been tempered, however, by the reascendancy of core knowledge (led by supporters of discipline initiation and citizenship education), as well as the criticisms of educational commentators who call for the return of back-to-basics education and a renewed emphasis on educational accountability via standardized testing (Chapter 6).

In inquiry learning classrooms, students draw maps, design charts, and build graphs as they study places both near and far. They map the school playground, conduct archeological digs, and go on walking trips in the local community. They rotate between learning centers, each of which teaches or reinforces one or more geographic skills and/or topics under study. They coplan units with teachers, follow their interests in researching esoteric and faraway places, and work in groups to prepare literature reviews and problem solve real-world geographic challenges. They likely work within a whole language context that celebrates authorship and leads students through the stages of writing, peer editing, publishing, and sharing their published works. They learn cooperative group work skills as they complete research projects in teams. Many of these activities are undoubtedly also to be found in classrooms that advocate a disciplinary initiation or citizenship education focus, but inquiry learning supporters celebrate these methodological approaches in and of themselves, rather than primarily relying on them as engaging pathways for transferring prescribed disciplinary or cultural knowledge.

The centrality of individual experience in inquiry learning marks an important shift in the student's acquisition of knowledge. This shift separates both this and the orientations discussed below from the disciplinary initiation and citizenship education positions reviewed above. Knowledge, in the eyes of inquiry learning supporters, neither exclusively resides within the domain of professionals (disciplinary initiation), nor does it comprise a set of permanent values that can be transmitted explicitly to students (citizenship education); rather, knowledge and values are contextual, evolving and changing over time, and individually and culturally constructed by both children and adults alike.

It follows from this that the study of *context* is an important theme within the study of place in this philosophy. Teachers capitalize on children's interest in the new and "esoteric" as they involve students in studies of faraway places and times (e.g., Ancient Egypt and Medieval civilizations). Microspaces and astronomy are studied for the unique perspectives—small and large—they offer students. Values clarification activities challenge students to think critically about the values they hold in relation to changing social contexts. Guided fantasy journeys aim to evoke students' imaginations and strengthen their sense of imagined places. Place education, within this context, posits something of a holistic curriculum and aims to connect with students' emotional and social lives, in addition to their cognitive lives.

There is a caveat to the above. Not all educators who teach within the inquiry learning tradition favor such holistic and nonanalytic approaches to the study of place. Many instead ally themselves (at least methodologically) to the disciplinary initiation philosophy. It is the scientific method, argue pragmatic educators, that provides the overarching framework upon which an ever-changing world can best be understood and values held in check (Dewey, 1916/1966). Working from the experiential learning context described above, students move through a problem-solving process that comprises the formation of hypotheses in response to problematic or experimental situations, the gathering of information, the testing of possible solutions, and the implementation and evaluating of such solutions in real-world contexts.

DEVELOPMENTAL CONGRUENCY

In the last chapter, it was lamented that while developmental theorists have posited a rich variety of models to explain the development of place perception in childhood, little of this research has in fact been applied to the way that the concept of place is studied in schools. Many teachers who support the inquiry learning philosophy also pride themselves in designing instructional programs for social studies and geography which honor student interests, aptitudes, and learning styles. It is rare, however, for even progressive educators to go one step further in addressing children's sensibilities by taking their pedagogical cues from what developmental researchers have gleaned about children's experience of place at various age levels. Little, if any, attention is paid to how children's perceptions of immediate and distant places change over time; still less to the ways in which younger and older children go about constructing their own place worlds in their daily lives.

In recent years, a few lone educators and researchers have attempted to address this omission, but the developmentally congruent approaches to the study of place that they advocate are by far the least well known and established of the pedagogical strategies reviewed in this chapter. Despite paying lip service to designing curriculum that is responsive to children's developmental experience, most educational programs only skim the service when it comes to teaching in a developmentally congruent way. A focus on transmitting core content and prescribed educational outcomes increasingly rules the day. Yet place study within a developmentally congruent context requires teachers and curriculum designers to clear their minds of any prescribed agenda and instead start where children are at, how they see the world, how they construct space, and how they deal with abstract spaces that lie beyond their immediate lived experience.

Consider the example of mapmaking. Is mapmaking a geographic tool or a window into the formative place-making world of childhood? For the advocates of the three philosophies reviewed thus far, mapmaking is first and foremost a skill that can assist students in organizing and communicating the geographic data they have researched and collected. Completed maps of the neighborhood, state, nation, and world (the scale of place is a nonissue) serve as public documents that are ideally navigable quite independently of the map's creator. So, too, well-drawn maps conform to the design standards established by professional (i.e., adult) geographers.

Mapmaking from a developmentally congruent point of view takes a markedly different route. Mapmaking is viewed not solely as a skill and tool, but more importantly as a developmental expression of the child's innermost need to organize, make sense of and connect with her surroundings. In much the same way that the narrative mode underlies a child's temporal strivings for order (Hutchison, 1998), mapmaking exercises a child's spatial modalities as he or she searches for a working theory of how the world works:

> One can think of mapmaking as a fundamental human activity . . . Learning consists of looking at something new and beginning to see paths into it. You construct a map or a series of maps, each one an approximation and probably wrong in many details, but each one helping you to go further into the territory . . . We all have hundreds, thousands of maps each of which represents a way we have learned to look at part of the world . . . There are music maps, language maps, maps of social relations, maps of the physical environment . . . What they have in common is that all of them are models in our minds of what we think the world looks like. (Kallett, 1995, pp. 3–4)

Whether maps are written down or mentally constructed in the mind, they serve the same purpose: to assist both children and adults in orienting themselves to the world. A child's map of the real world very likely focuses on what the child already knows firsthand: his or her home, neighborhood, play area, route to school, and so forth. (Such maps may well be complemented by hand-drawn fantasy maps featuring mythical places inspired by a child's imagination and treasured storybooks.) Mapmaking, from this perspective, is deeply personal and very often related to the significant places in a child's life. Spaces that afford privacy, secret meeting places for friends, found objects (both natural and humanmade), and pathways to here and there are plotted, coveted, and referenced in relation to home.

When given the choice, children are likely to pass up opportunities to draw maps of real-world large-scale regions that can only be known on an abstract level (e.g., state, country, and world). They instead favor the invitation to draw maps of familiar places: their home, neighborhood, and play areas. Far from being public documents, the maps that children *freely* draw are very often topographic narratives that tell the story of a child's discovery of a favorite place. So, too, from a developmental perspective, the design of children's maps conforms less to the professional geographic standards established by adults and more to children's unique perceptual, spatial, and emotionally resonant ways of perceiving the world around them at various ages.

In his book *Mapmaking with Children*, David Sobel (1998) calls for a developmentally congruent transformation in the way geography is taught in elementary school. Sobel laments the fact that "world maps are foisted onto first graders who barely have a sense of their own neighborhood" (p. 10). He further advises teachers that:

> We do a disservice to children when we jump in too quickly at a prema-turely abstract level in map reading and mapmaking. It's important to have children begin mapmaking the way they begin drawing: maps and drawings are representations of things that are emotionally important to children. In the beginning, children's maps represent their experiences of beauty, secrecy, adventure, and comfort. With these affective endeavors as a foundation, I then gradually start to focus on scale, location, direction, and geographic relationships. The development of emotional bonds *and* cognitive skills needs to go hand in hand in my approach to developmentally appropriate social studies and geography. (p. 5)

For Sobel, a developmentally congruent approach to the study of place proceeds not from a state-mandated curriculum, nor from a study of faraway or large-scale places that can only be known on an abstract level, but rather from the teacher's careful analysis of children's maps of immediate vicinities. By analyzing children's neighborhood maps (much as they already analyze children's writing) teachers can construct a de-velopmental model of children's place-making strivings at various ages and then apply what they have learned to the design of a developmen-tally responsive social studies and geography curriculum. Sobel charts the path by which children mature from pictorial and home-centered maps (ages 5 to 6) through to neighborhood maps incorporating dimen-sionality, pathways, and special places (ages 7 to 8); and on to abstract, aerial, and wide-area maps incorporating both residential and business districts (ages 11 to 12). He outlines in detail a wide variety of mapmaking activities that both complement and nurture children's place-making abilities as they mature throughout middle childhood.

COMMUNITY STUDY

Honoring a young student's inner motivations and developing cognitive structures of mind constitutes a developmental approach to place study built on the premise that formal learning should connect with children's place experiences in the real world. The cultural equivalent to this developmental focus on childhood might well be community study, which takes its cue not from the child but rather the immediate cultural universe within which the child lives and, however subconsciously, identifies.

Many school districts incorporate a cursory study of the local community early in the primary years prior to introducing regional, national, and world geography. This strategy arises out of an *expanding horizons* approach to social studies. Young children initially study the immediate, familiar, and concrete (e.g., self, family, and neighborhood), but quickly work their way outward to focus on the wider geographic regions of state, country, and world.

Unfortunately, most primary-level community study units tend to be generic and cursory. More often than not, it is the metastructure of a typical community (e.g., community helpers and buildings) that is introduced to students rather than those features and amenities that are unique to the specific community within which students live. Moreover, by the time students have reached an age where they are ready to engage in a more in-depth study of their local community, the community study unit of the primary years is long forgotten, never to be returned to, in favor of a focus on state, national, and world geography.

Advocates of community study lament the opportunities that are lost in failing to return to a more in-depth study of the local community in the upper elementary, secondary, and postsecondary grades (Orr, 1992; Theobald, 1997). Within this philosophy, the local community—whether it be a metropolitan city, a small town, a village, or a farming community—is viewed as an ecosystem with feedback connections that integrate the infrastructure of the community, its institutions, market economies, cultural groups, and other features with the natural and built environments that define the community's living space. Community study advocates argue that learning how communities function as ecosystems can help students to appreciate more fully the biological and cultural interdependencies that sustain their living space and the living space of others (including other species). To know one's place is to have an intimate knowledge of the local environment (both natural and built) and the various professional roles, shared histories, and interdependent relationships that sustain the community over the long term.

Through the study of the local community, data gathering, interviewing, and other research skills are learned and practiced. Folktales and historic records are compiled. Paintings by local artists, old photographs, monuments, the architectural stylings of local buildings, and other artifacts are analyzed for common or divergent threads of meaning. In ethnically diverse communities, the multicultural experience of place is deepened through visits to settings that incorporate a variety of architectural styles and cultural icons. The environmental health of the local community and the ecological characteristics of the wider bioregion are investigated. Excursions outside the school are complemented with visits to the school by adult role models who perform key roles in sustaining the physical and cultural infrastructure of the community. City maps are used to teach mapping skills. Historical maps and aerial photographs track urbanization patterns over time. The underside of the city (i.e., below street level) is studied. Transportation routes are plotted, as are the flow of electricity, water, and sewage. The study of the flow of energy and waste products through the local community introduces students to the basic principles of environmental and community economics.

The Common Roots program, a Vermont-based ecoliteracy initiative (Food Works, 1992), provides a good example of community study in practice. Elementary school children grow "historical theme gardens" and learn about the various cultural and historical practices that connect the themes of food, community, and ecology. In going beyond a traditional school gardening strategy (such as that described in Chapter 4), the Common Roots program contextualizes children's gardening endeavors within the study of the local bioregion, folklore, and community history. By focusing on food as an ecological, as well as cultural system of exchanges, students in this program make connections between the ecological practice of gardening and the cultural/historical practices of growing, preparing, and sharing/selling food.

Most community study initiatives aim to nurture in students a deep-seated appreciation for how their communities work. Some projects, however, also incorporate a *social action* agenda that encourages students to actively make a difference in their local community by improving it in some meaningful way. The Saginaw River Project in Michigan (Pelkki, 1994) is a good example of such an initiative. Responding to health concerns regarding the water quality of the Saginaw River, elementary and secondary school students began conducting regular water quality tests of the river in 1989. Their results showed an alarmingly high fecal coliform count that soon led public health officials to institute new safety measures for use of the river.

Had the Saginaw project ended there, it would have already made an important contribution to improving the public health of the local community. However, as the project moved forward, teachers began to find new learning possibilities that emerged out of a broader view of the cultural and ecological interdependencies that connected the river to the local community:

> As the project to test the river progressed, the teachers . . . began to see the River Project in different ways. Why not look at the river not only as a geographic entity, but also as a factor in the history, politics, culture, commerce, and recreation of our city? . . . [Soon] students [were going] to the library to read about the history of the city and how the river affected the development of our community. They talked to local historians and history buffs and went on to write stories, poems, and other accounts. (Pelkki, 1994, p. 32)

This project originally began as a simple water quality initiative, but soon blossomed into an interdisciplinary project that connected the diverse subject areas of ecology, natural history, environmental activism, and media literacy. Among the outcomes of the project are a series of poetry books, a 1-hour video documentary, and regular "rivercasts" that report biweekly on the continuing successes of the project.

GLOBAL EDUCATION

Teaching in a developmentally congruent way was linked earlier in this chapter to the study of children's immediate surroundings, but a developmentally congruent approach to the study of place can start on either of two scales—children's experience of their immediate surroundings, or their understandings of faraway places (Wiegand, 1992). Both starting points trace their roots not to specific locales, but rather to the consciousness of the individual child who ascribes meaning to both the nearby places she encounters in daily life and the faraway places she vicariously learns about through interactions with adults, peers, media, and the wider cultural universe.

Global educators are concerned with the larger of these two scales and many are particularly concerned with the stereotypes, prejudices, and disconnections to faraway places that children often pick up from the immediate cultural universe that embeds their lives. In seeking to nurture a deeper sense of international understanding in students, global educators aim to complement (and, indeed, sometimes counter) through international education the citizenship education students receive as they study their home country.

Whatever their specific topic focus, global educators are united in the view that we live in an increasingly interdependent world that eclipses the myopic attention that has historically been paid to the nation-state as the governing context for place study in schools. Societal, economic, technological, and political shifts in the cultural makeup of nations, the rise of transnational corporations and globalized trade relationships, advances in travel and telecommunications, and the ascendancy of international institutions, including the United Nations and World Bank, have each contributed, along with numerous other forces, to the formation of an interconnected and globalized world that directly impacts on the lives of *all* peoples regardless of nationality.

Despite a general agreement with the above, the gulf between competing definitions of global education is almost as wide as the scale of place that global educators seek to privilege. At one end of the spectrum is what might best be described as global education for transnational business opportunities—the noncritical, economic-driven notion that in an increasingly globalized world students require a solid understanding of the cultural and economic characteristics of America's major trading partners, as well as emerging markets around the world. At the other end of the spectrum is a critical sociological approach to global education which seeks to expose disparities and inequities in the living conditions, economic prospects, and distribution of privilege and power between people in developed and developing nations (Pike & Selby, 1991).

Complementing the economic focus of the above two philosophies are numerous other global education approaches, including comparative education, development education, environmental education, human rights education, multicultural education, and peace education. Each claims a specific piece of the global education pie, so to speak, but all are united in the view that only a wide-scale vision of the world can provide students with a full understanding of their place within the world. On the face of it, this notion would seem to contrast quite sharply with the community study philosophy reviewed earlier, but the differences between these two visions of place education are potentially made mute by the axiom "think global, act local." Working within a social action context, many educators encourage students to glean what they can from their study of global education in order to make a difference in their local communities.

The argument for an expanding horizons approach to social studies, the notion of beginning with the local and gradually expanding outward, was discussed earlier in this chapter. The contrasting position arises within a global education context and provides first-grade students with a view of the Earth (or solar system) as a single entity and only gradually zooms in to provide a level of detail that differentiates between the Earth's constituent physical regions, continents, political boundaries, and so forth. This contrasting vision of place aims to present the Earth to the young child as a unified whole, as a shared planet of many peoples (and species) who hold much in common with one another, including a shared home:

> What is this World Core Curriculum? Simply stated its objectives are to give children: 1) a good picture of the home into which they are born—from the infinitely large realm of the universe and our planetary home down to the atom and the infinitely small; 2) a correct picture of the family into which they are born—namely, the human family with its great variety of natural and culturally common features and infinite diversity; 3) an accurate picture of the time flow into which they are born—from paleontology, archaeology, and history to the future; and 4) a sense of their important, personal, miraculous lives in this wondrous creation, with the physical, mental, sentimental, and spiritual qualities, and the role they can play to further humanity's progress during their life on earth. (Muller, 1989, p. 284)

It may at first seem ironic, but it is the critics of global education (of which there are many) who arguably provide the most revealing, if overtly partisan, view of the construction of place in this philosophy (Gaddy et al., 1996). Working from a religious fundamentalist perspective, some critics have openly challenged global education's tendency to privilege international institutions (leading to world government, it is charged) over the sovereign right of nations to chart their own pathways into the future:

> The depreciation of America and the proclamation of the globalist view of peace are programming children to accept four New Age goals: 1) a New World Order, which implies a one-world government; 2) a new world religion. The New Age medley (syncretism) of humanism, Hinduism, and every other religion—except genuine Christianity—fits the bill perfectly; 3) a new economic system to redistribute the world's wealth—especially America's; and 4) a spiritually evolved global citizenry ruled by the most advanced and most aware. (Kjos, 1990, p. 61)

Critics react with dismay to the assertion that global education has the potential to "be an important factor in helping the world make a more or less smooth transition from nationalism to a more integrated global society" (Tye, 1999, p. 13). Such thinking, they charge, strikes at the heart of the citizenship education philosophy upon which American education has been built. In the eyes of fundamentalist critics in particular, global education disenfranchises Western civilization, Judeo-Christian values, and pride in nation by preaching a form of global contextualism and anti-Christian secular humanism in which all values are equal and no values are absolute (Buehrer, 1990). The result is the loss of a common cultural vocabulary and set of shared cultural sensibilities potentially leading to a full-scale loss of nationhood.

Global educators would no doubt wish to challenge their critics on each of these points but, for the purpose of this chapter, it is the discourse itself that sharply delineates the major pedagogical differences to be found in the way in which pedagogy and place is constructed by these and the other philosophies reviewed above.

TEACHING ACROSS THE PHILOSOPHIES

There are probably few teachers who subscribe to any one of the above philosophies exclusively. No doubt, too, there are many premises tied to competing philosophies which resonate with readers. After all, each of these six orientations does have its own unique merit and appeal. This begs the question, Can educators not teach across two or more philosophies, incorporating elements of multiple positions into their educational practice? I will close this chapter by briefly considering two such examples of cross-orientation teaching.

Disciplinary Initiation and Developmental Congruency

There is an inherent tension between the disciplinary initiation and developmental congruency philosophies that extends from the conflicting goals each posits for place education, particularly in early and middle childhood. Disciplinary initiation, on the one hand, seeks to dispel students' mythic and untested convictions and belief systems about how the world works by situating the formal study of place within a tested and culturally established disciplinary context. So, too, the mapping and geography skills that students learn in this tradition extend from the very same skill sets employed by professional geographers.

Advocates of developmental congruency, on the other hand, look to the individual child's developmental experience and readiness in constructing a place curriculum. To attempt to supplant a child's developmentally congruent way of envisioning place with an imposed formalized view of place is to risk creating a disconnection between the way that children are required to make sense of place in school and the way they freely choose to construct place outside of school, in the real world, where deeply held place sensibilities can be safely fallen back on.

To teach across the disciplinary initiation and developmental congruency orientations perhaps requires a teacher to view a child's ingrained and deeply held view of place as a necessary—developmental advocates would say *privileged*—starting point for formal education and a mature disciplinary understanding of place as the desired end goal. Time is an ally in this regard, for as children grow and develop, so too do their deeply held understandings of the world. Learning within a combined disciplinary initiation and developmental congruency approach likely involves taking advantage of the cognitive disequilibrium that may arise when students encounter phenomena that are best explained using disciplinary or evidentiary means. Yet lest the march toward disciplinary education proceed too fast, advocates of developmental congruency are apt to caution teachers that they still risk creating a disconnect between formal education (i.e., How I am required to construct place in school?) and day-to-day living (i.e., How do I choose to navigate the places I inhabit when not in school?).

Mythic sensibilities about place and how the world works more generally are surprisingly resilient and very often held by people well into adulthood regardless of completed level of education or profession (Gardner, 1991). Although they may well be misguided and wrongheaded, such mythic sensibilities nevertheless serve both children and adults as functional means for making one's way through the world in daily life. If it is a goal of formal education to supplant these mythic sensibilities in favor of a tested disciplinary understanding of the world then it may well be necessary that the formal study of place in early and middle childhood begin not with a disciplinary understanding of place, but rather with where children are at, how they conceive of and make sense of place and the world more generally.

Citizenship Education and Global Education

There are at least two pathways by which citizenship education and global education can each contribute to a common vision of place in schools. The first pathway is noncritical and was noted earlier in relation to both citizenship and global education. In keeping with the citizenship focus on nationhood, other countries can be studied in relation to the home country through cross-cultural comparative analyses of political systems and cultural traditions plus international studies related to the flow of goods and people between nations. Likewise, major trading partners and emerging world markets can be studied for the future advantage they provide students with regard to forging strong economic ties with businesses in other countries.

The other and far more controversial pathway problematizes the home country in light of the wider global context and calls into question specific national values, policies, and practices that arguably serve (intended or not) to disenfranchise people, species, and natural environments outside of the home country. At the heart of this pathway are some difficult questions: Is it an oxymoron for a person to claim patriotism while simultaneously being critical of one's home country? Does enlightened patriotism itself imply a healthy skepticism of one's home country, a stepping back, so to speak, to take into account how one's home country is viewed and experienced from afar, if only for the sake of improving the home country's standing in the world? The answers to these (and many other related) questions are of course open to (heated) debate and they are perhaps of particular relevance to the United States given this country's standing as the only remaining superpower in the world. At the heart of the debate between global education and its critics is a delicate balancing act between nationalism and globalism, national sovereignty and an increasingly interdependent world. Perhaps it is *this* debate itself that should constitute the study of place in the upper elementary and secondary grades as students engage each other in a critical and disciplined discourse that addresses the merits of both the citizenship and global education philosophies.

Chapter 3

ARCHITECTURAL AND
DESIGN PERSPECTIVES

*It would seem logical to design school buildings by considering current
issues in education and new developments in curriculum. . . . But current
volatile issues in education will soon become historical, and new trends will
inevitably continue to arise. Buildings endure, and they must be able to
serve changing needs over long periods, or they will quickly become
obsolete. This suggests that we need to plan learning environments around
foundational issues rather than current events—around basic understandings
of children, how they learn, and most important, how their environment
can enhance those learnings.*
—Elizabeth Hebert (1992, p. 34)

What impact does the physical design of a school have on the quality of
instruction that occurs in a classroom? At one extreme is the view that
the educational setting is of little relevance to the teaching and learning
process. All that is required is a teacher, a student, and a log for both to sit
on, argued C. D. Lewis in 1937. At the other extreme is a fixation on the
conveniences, design fads, and technological amenities of modern educational settings, which can sometimes overshadow the attention that is paid
to how these amenities actually contribute to the teaching and learning
process.

To retrace the history of school design in the United States is to follow the intersection of architectural style, educational philosophy, demographics, and budgetary realities through time. Some clear trends emerge:
Over the last few centuries, class sizes in state schools have fallen sharply
from hundreds of students to several dozen students, resulting in more
classrooms per school. Flexibility in classroom design and seating arrange-
ments have emerged as important considerations in the planning of
schools. The creation of communal areas, such as gymnasiums, staff
rooms, and other meeting places has given rise to the specialization of
spaces in schools (Rieselbach, 1990). A concern for the school as a public

institution has led to design initiatives that promote the public use of educational facilities by local residents—students and nonstudents alike.

The earliest schools (in the modern age) were run by churches. Prior to such initiatives, affluent children were tutored in their homes. Less well-off children, if they received any formal instruction at all, organized their own education on a per community basis. Of the first attempts at a state-run, public system of education, it is the 19th-century one-room schoolhouse—some 400 were still in operation in the U.S. in 2000 (U.S. Department of Education, 2001)—that retains a special significance in the eyes of many. The one-room schoolhouse (see Figure 3.1), with its multigrade classroom and rote system of instruction, symbolized the early promise of a public and democratic system of education. In many towns and villages, it was the church, with its protruding steeple, and the school, with its distinctive bell tower (see Figure 3.2), that functioned at the social (and often political) center of town life.

FIGURE 3.1. A prominently placed bell and a wood-burning stove mark one of the oldest one-room school buildings in Ontario (situated in the historic community of St. John's).

FIGURE 3.2. Opened in 1920, Ridgeway Public School (District School Board of Niagara, Ontario) proudly displays an historic bell tower that denotes its privileged place at the center of town life.

During this early period, perhaps the most important change in public education, from an architectural standpoint, was the gradual shift from a nongraded, one-room schoolhouse to a multigrade and, therefore, multiclassroom school. This was necessitated by a rising population, growing patterns of urbanization, an increasingly divergent school curriculum, and the influx of a wider age range of students into schools.

The designs of the first multigrade public schools conformed to the instructional philosophies and educational practices of the time, a reflexive tendency that has continued to this day. Boston's Quincy Grammar School, built in 1848, was typical of the period. The four-story building housed some 650 students and included a basement and attic (Graves, 1993). The first three stories housed the 12 classrooms, each opening up into a common hallway, while the fourth floor hosted an assembly hall that could seat the entire student body. Individual desks for each student—an important innovation for the time—were bolted to the floor. The seating arrangement in rows supported the transmission and rote teaching approaches that were in near universal use.

With few exceptions, this basic plan for the design of self-contained classrooms, each opening up into a common corridor, continues to be the most prominent design philosophy at work in schools today. Although punctured by occasional forays into more radical design initiatives, school planning, particularly until the late 1930s, embraced a nationwide mono-theism that Ben E. Graves (1993, p. 25) characterizes as "a brick box with holes for windows in a style that can only be described as neutered."

Although the exterior design and general layout of schools remained stagnant throughout the first decades of the 20th century, the interior design of classrooms underwent several reforms. The first decades of the 20th century were marked by the rise of progressive education. Embracing the scientific and democratic optimism of the day, progressive educators argued for the need to foster an experimental temperament in students and incorporate more participatory approaches to learning in schools. In response to these pronouncements, the interior design of schools was transformed to accommodate the new instructional approaches that were quickly gaining support. Desks were unbolted from floors. Open areas were created in classrooms for collaborative student work. Closet space for storing teaching apparatus and other materials became an important design consideration as the principle of "learning by doing" took hold. Child-centered (and child-scaled) learning environments were introduced. Specialty rooms for so-called nonacademic subjects, such as music, athletics, and industrial arts, made their first appearance. Improvements to the basic infrastructure of schools, particularly in terms of heating, lighting, bathroom facilities, and other health and safety factors were implemented.

Insofar as it was educational ideology that influenced school design in the early decades of the 20th century, it was the sheer rapidity of changes to the demographics of the post–World War II period that ushered in the modern age of school design. The end of the Second World War marked the beginning of the baby-boom generation and educational planners responded to the impending influx of children into the educational system with a flurry of school construction that was unprecedented in the history of education. In the late 1960s and early 1970s, even ambitious school construction efforts had trouble meeting the accommodation needs of an exploding school-aged population. Many communities adopted a prefabricated assembly approach to school construction or purchased and renovated existing spaces in factories, supermarkets, and retail malls to expand their educational programs. So, too, ambitious experimental plans for schools were encouraged, most notably by the Educational Facilities Laboratories, which supported movable wall and open plan designs, as well as early new media ventures (Brubaker, 1998). Yet the influx of children into the school system was not to last. By the mid-1970s, the school-aged population in the United States had begun to subside and many communities began selling off unused schools to cope with the budgetary realities associated with declining school enrollments.

THE MODEL SCHOOL

During the heyday of the school construction craze in the 1950s and 1960s, there was one school that epitomized for many the transition to the modern age of school design. Crow Island Elementary School, which opened its doors in Winnetka, Illinois in 1940, marked an early effort to design a school that was both innovative for its time and consciously responsive to the needs of the children and educators who would populate its halls for years to come. The single-story school, which houses some 350 students, was planned with collaboration in mind and it was only after an extended period of consultation with educators, designers, and other stakeholders that construction began. The following letter written in 1938 to the architects from a creative activities teacher foreshadows much of the aesthetic character that was to find its way into the final design of the school:

> The building must not be too beautiful, lest it be a place for children to keep and not one for them to use. The materials must be those not easily marred, and permitting of some abuse. The finish and settings must form a harmonious background [to] honest child effort and creation, not one which will make children's work seem crude. Above all, the school must be child-like, not what adults think of children. . . . It must be warm, personal, and intimate, that it shall be to thousands of children through the years "my school." (As quoted in Presler, 1992, pp. 59–60)

The architects of Crow Island Elementary School took their cue from the above and other visions put forward by members of the Winnetka school community. The Crow Island alternative did away with the imposing Victorian-inspired scale of traditional school design. Gone was the brick-box architecture and rigid egg-carton organization of classrooms into discrete learning cells. Instead, the architects adopted a residentially scaled and informal, but carefully crafted, design that housed L-shaped classrooms in separate grade-level wings, each with its own distinctive character (Graves, 1993). In an effort to make the school child-scaled, light switches and other interface elements were placed at lower than normal levels. Ceilings were made 9 feet high, rather than the more traditional but imposing 12 feet. In order to complement the building's aesthetic character and child-scaled goals, the architects also designed the furniture for the school. In a nod to the historic role of schools as the center of town life, Crow Island features a clock tower that is positioned just slightly off center so as to underscore the nonformal design considerations at work.

In an effort to affect a seamless transition between the school and the world outside, the unopposing design plan for Crow Island was complemented by the use of natural lighting, including skylights and large wall windows judiciously placed throughout the school. In reflecting on his design work for Crow Island and other schools, Lawrence B. Perkins (1957) comments on the contrasting character of natural versus traditional lighting in schools:

> Lighting can make the classroom come alive. . . . Naturally, the first job is to provide proper seeing conditions, but this is not the only goal. Lighting must also contribute to the mood for learning, to the psychological well-being of the student. It must be a stimulant. Bland, coldly uniform, "scientifically-planned" lighting usually has the opposite effect: It bores and depresses. A clue to the best answer can perhaps be found in the lighting of the fields and forests, where the eye evolved. So, too, the classroom can have a lighting that changes, that is a shifting interplay of opposites—warm and cool, light and shadow, soft and hard, level light, and accent light. This will give the interest and the stimulation that make the classroom a place to enjoy, an agreeable place to work and learn. (p. 37)

At its heart, the Crow Island design exemplifies Friedrich Froebel's 19th century vision of the school as "a garden of children." Wherever possible, natural elements are used to complement and augment the built environment of the school. In addition to incorporating natural lighting, each classroom opens directly into an outside courtyard. So, too, the exterior and interior rose-colored brick walls of the school are trimmed with redwood and Ponderosa pine, respectively. In a truly nontraditional move, three fireplaces adorn the school to create a welcoming and homey milieu.

Crow Island School was designated a national historic landmark in 1990 and has been twice nominated (in polls conducted by the *Architectural Record*) as one of the most important buildings designed in the United States in the last 100 years. In 1990, a group of educators and architects gathered at the school to celebrate its 50th anniversary and renew their commitment to innovative and educationally responsive approaches to school design.

CURRENT TRENDS AND INFLUENCES

Crow Island School is undoubtedly one of the most honored public school buildings of the 20th century, but do the design considerations that contribute to its historic prestige also underscore the design principles at work in newly built schools today? A brief survey of a number of current school design trends and influences suggests that while some aspects of Crow Island School may continue to be favored by school architects, other, even more critical, issues associated with changing societal, economic, and technological conditions are also, out of necessity, getting attention.

Budgetary Realities

At the beginning of the 21st century, the same forces that contributed to rising school enrollments in the 1950s and 1960s, namely increases in the birth rates in the United States, now coupled with the rise of the immigrant populations in large urban centers, have once again resulted in the need for new schools. Today, however, the public seems wary of ambitious but expensive school construction projects. Gone is the implicit optimism of the postwar period and the public's infinite faith in the ability of public education to ensure equality of opportunity and a prosperous future for all. Throughout the last 2 decades, we have witnessed a flurry of criticisms against the merits of public education and particularly its excesses in so-called nonacademic areas, and this has taken its toll on public support for ambitious but costly school reform projects.

So, too, the public purse is no longer what it once was. As the school-aged population grew throughout the 1950s and 1960s, so did the populations of urban and suburban areas, resulting in an ever-expanding real estate tax base (Cook, 1996). Today, however, a general tax malaise has set in and this, coupled with an aging population with few direct ties to public education, has left many communities with limited capital budgets for school construction projects. Hence there is a need to reframe the priorities of school design so as to garner public support and ensure efficiency of operation.

Community Use Initiatives

How are schools to cope with the reality of declining school construction budgets at a time when school enrollment is on the rise? A popular tactic has been to try and win back public support for educational building expenditures by extending the services offered by schools to adults in the local community. Many schools have instituted community use policies in which selected spaces within schools, such as recreational areas, library/media centers, and auditoriums are available for day and/or evening use by both individuals and community organizations. As well, some schools share their space with a local community center, child care program, or public library. Finally, many schools now offer adult education classes in addition to their regular programs for children. In addition to bringing in extra revenue, community use initiatives and adult education courses also help to strengthen a school's connection to the local community and build goodwill with neighborhood residents.

Clearly, a community use policy cannot be implemented overnight. There are administrative, policy, and personnel questions that need to be considered, but so, too, there are school design issues that also need to be addressed. Once a school begins to cater to the needs of the wider community of adult residents, concerns for the safety of students and staff, the increasing flow of traffic through the school, and the extra wear and tear on the school building itself begin to arise. To deal with these challenges, many schools have adopted a strategic zoning approach to managing school facilities. Certain areas in the school are designated as being for public use and others are for the use of students and staff exclusively. In newly designed schools, public areas tend to be clustered together and situated close to the main entrance to the school. This allows for better control over the comings and goings of individuals and permits better evening access.

When fully embraced, community use initiatives and other efforts to improve the relevancy of schools to the local community have the potential to restore the historic 19th century role of the school as the social center of town life. (Such initiatives may also help to strengthen support for a public school's right to exist at a time when calls for the privatization of all things public, the focus of Chapter 6, are gaining momentum.) Indeed, the trend to adopt community use policies in schools is likely to grow, not diminish, in the coming years. Were it not for the community use initiatives which are being put into practice today, many of the schools that have been constructed in recent years could well be empty by the second or third decades of the 21st century as school enrollment once again begins to decline.

Accessibility

In addition to instituting community use policies, many school districts have also endeavored to broaden access to schools in another important way. One of the consequences of new building codes and the current effort to fully integrate students with physical handicaps and other exceptionalities into regular classrooms has been a series of design initiatives for improving the accessibility of new schools and existing facilities that undergo renovations.

Proponents of the integration (or mainstreaming) movement in special education argue that the traditional practice of segregating exceptional students from their peers adversely affects children's social development and level of self-esteem. Segregation practices are also judged to be an equity issue in which exceptional children are denied the same academic experiences and opportunities for advancement as children without handicaps. Many school administrators cite similar reasons for supporting integration practices, but there are also budgetary realities that make segregated special education services costly to provide. Hence, most school districts now integrate students with mild to moderate special needs into regular classrooms on a full- or part-time basis. Where necessary, exceptional students are provided with additional remedial services and other supports that complement the regular classroom program.

Among the many design initiatives for improving accessibility are handicapped parking spaces; wheelchair ramps; wide entrances and aisles; elevators for multistory school buildings; accessible bathrooms; and lowered blackboards, light switches, and other control mechanisms (Kowalski, 1989). Attention also needs to be paid to the design of the school furniture. Tables, for example, tend to be too low to accommodate wheelchairs. Likewise, lecture halls and auditoriums with fixed seating require open spaces for accommodating wheelchairs. For people with acute visual or auditory exceptionalities, redundant visual and auditory cues (e.g., for fire alarms) are also important design considerations.

Specialty Schools

At the same time as the integration movement gains ground in its effort to equalize the education that children receive, there is also an effort underway to build specialized educational spaces that emphasize a particular subject focus or teaching methodology (see Figure 3.3). Throughout the last half century there have been at least three waves of specialty school reform in North America. During the 1950s and 1960s, in an effort to break traditional patterns of racial segregation, many large urban centers in the United States opened magnet schools, educational facilities that incorporated a unique subject focus and brought together students from all around a given city. Throughout the late 1960s and early 1970s, public alternative schools (such as the School for Experiential Education, noted in the Introduction) gained increasing favor among students by embracing a more democratic approach to education. Beginning in the 1980s, there was a significant rise in the number of specialty schools that emphasized a unique

FIGURE 3.3. Specialized learning settings, such as this secondary school's auto body shop, challenge our stereotypical notions of classroom design.

subject focus, such as the arts, science and technology, second-language immersion, business, or environmental studies. The last few years have also seen new specialty schools that emphasize a back-to-basics approach to instruction. Some of these schools cater to male or female students exclusively.

Some specialty schools are housed in their own school building, while others share their school space with that of a traditional school, essentially functioning as a school within a school (Brubaker, 1998). Many specialty schools have unique design requirements related to their particular subject focus or instructional methodology. Performance art schools, for example, have professional stage, sound, and lighting requirements. Science schools, on the other hand, have special laboratory and equipment needs. (A Toronto secondary school with a specialized microbiology program could boast as early as the mid-1980s that it housed the only electron microscope in a Canadian public school, for example.) As will be made clear in the next chapter certain schools that embrace a unique instructional philosophy may also choose to infuse that particular philosophy into the design of the school itself.

Multipurpose Spaces/Expandability

Historically, the design of educational facilities incorporated clear and recognizable areas, each of which served a single purpose. Today, however, seemingly compatible areas of a school, such as the library and computer lab, are just as likely to be combined in order to ensure the efficient use of space and reduce overall construction and maintenance costs. (Moving the computer lab into the library does, however, risk a loss of commitment to print resources as shelf space and book buying budgets are reallocated to make way for computer hardware and software.) This multipurpose strategy also extends to underutilized areas of schools. Consider, for example, the auditorium and cafeteria spaces in many secondary schools. To function effectively, both areas require a large allotment of space, which is then likely to be used only sporadically throughout the day. Although scheduling conflicts may well arise (Paire, 1998), some secondary school designers have opted to combine these two spaces in order to ensure efficiency of operation and reduce overall construction costs.

Hugh Cook (1996), in taking this example a step further, distinguishes between two approaches for combining the auditorium and cafeteria areas of schools. Both strategies are selectively being implemented in schools today. The *cafetorium* is a flexible, multiuse space that can be used either as a theater or dining area. Although its main function is as a cafeteria, the cafetorium is equipped with stage curtains, which can be concealed during dining hours, as well as a raised stage, portable seating, acoustical panels, and a pipe grid system for manipulating lighting, props, and scenery. From an opposite vantage point, the *auditoria* is designed to be used primarily as an auditorium for performances and assemblies, although it can also double as a dining hall. Auditorias are equipped with tiered flooring and more professional theatrical rigging, lighting, and sound systems than those to be found in cafetoriums.

In addition to incorporating multipurpose spaces, many new schools are also designed with future expandability in mind. The influx of immigrants into urban centers and ever-changing patterns of human migration between communities have made it difficult for school districts to make accurate long-term enrollment projections. In addition to portables and relocatable units (see Figure 3.4), school districts routinely rely on both attached and detached additions to existing school buildings (see Figure 3.5). In the mid- to late 1990s, additions and renovations to existing school

FIGURE 3.4. School districts are turning to portables to mitigate both declining school construction budgets and overpopulation in schools.

facilities accounted for just over 50% of the total monies spent on school construction in the United States (Perkins, 2001; U.S. General Accounting Office, 1997).

Year-Round Schooling/Energy Conservation

The traditional school year, which begins in September and ends in May or June, is currently being reevaluated in many communities as school districts look for ways to make more efficient use of school facilities throughout the entire calendar year, including the summer months. In many school districts, rising school enrollment coupled with finite school space has resulted in the need for a staggered approach to school use in which some students are in class while others are on vacation. A multi-track approach to year-round schooling (Shields, 2000) places groups of students and teachers in separate tracks, each of which has several sched-

FIGURE 3.5. Look closely at the exterior of a school and notice how its brickwork reveals a history of additions to the school building. Now venture inside and look for changing design philosophies.

uled learning rounds (e.g., 45 school days) marked off by short vacation breaks (e.g., 15 days). In addition to making more efficient use of school buildings, proponents of year-round schooling argue that students in a multitrack system also retain more of what they learn compared to students who each year take an extended 2- or 3-month summer vacation (Jacobs, 1998). Furthermore, the year-round approach to schooling is judged to be more conducive to contemporary lifestyle patterns and work habits. The traditional school year, on the other hand, is dismissed as conforming to a largely antiquated and agrarian calendar that is no longer relevant in most jurisdictions.

In terms of efficiency, year-round schooling is something of a double-edged sword. While this initiative may indeed make more efficient use of school space, consideration also needs to be given to energy use. Many year-round schools require both air-conditioning and heating systems.

Each uses considerable energy resources. Given the current budgetary realities, it is not surprising that many school districts are continually looking for more efficient energy use strategies. In the name of energy efficiency, new schools, year-round or otherwise (in sharp contrast to Crow Island School and other pre-energy crisis facilities), are increasingly closed off from the outside world. Windows are few and far between. Open ventilation to the air outside of the school is avoided.

School designers that can afford to have elected to install state-of-the-art environmental control systems to help further reduce expenditures associated with energy consumption. During the planning stages for new schools, low-tech solutions that optimally orient schools to the sun and/or incorporate natural lighting and ventilation strategies have also proven successful (MacKenzie, 1989).

Such initiatives may well be worth the effort. As early as the mid-1990s, the American Association of School Administrators estimated that an effective energy management policy for American schools could save taxpayers almost $2 billion annually (Graves, 1993). To support such conservation efforts, some schools have begun to conduct regular environmental audits that track the flow of energy and waste products through the school. In addition to promoting energy efficiency, such initiatives also have the potential to promote an environmental ethic in staff and students. Working with outside environmental organizations, such as Alberta, Canada's Environmental Resource Center, students, teachers, and custodial staff can track energy-use patterns related to heating, lighting, and electricity in their school. Results are then tallied and a "remedial action plan" is put into place to help further reduce energy consumption.

Technological Infrastructure

Without a doubt, the school design initiative that has received the most media attention in recent years is the current publicly and privately funded effort to modernize the technological infrastructure of schools throughout the United States. (This new technological mandate for schools is the focus of Chapter 5.) Since the mid-1990s, a growing number of school districts have sought to modernize the technical backbone of their educational facilities in an effort to provide Internet access to every classroom and networked access between computers in schools. Modernizing the technological infrastructure of schools requires the installation of computers, servers, and other hardware; the laying down of wiring and cables to connect the computers; and the installation of system, communication, and application software. (As this book goes to press, new wireless networking technologies are increasingly gaining favor and reducing the need to lay down physical cabling in schools. Some schools are opting to purchase, rent, or lease-to-own portable laptop computers, rather than having stationary desktop computers for students.) To support such initiatives, school districts throughout the United States and elsewhere in the world have organized "NetDays," short periods of intensive activity involving teachers, students, parents, technical experts, and volunteers aimed at installing the basic technical infrastructure needed by schools to provide Internet and networked access to classrooms. The NetDay (2003) Web site provides the following overview:

> NetDay is a historic grassroots effort in the classic American barn-raising tradition. Using volunteer labor, our goal is to lay all the basic wiring needed to make five classrooms and a library or computer lab in every school Internet-ready. If the same work were financed by taxpayers, it would cost more than $1,000 per classroom. Volunteers from businesses, education, and the community acquire all of the equipment and install and test it at every school site. . . . By bringing together these diverse elements, NetDay establishes a framework for lasting partnerships among business, government, educational institutions, and local communities to provide ongoing support for our schools.

Unlike most other design initiatives, costs associated with the wiring of schools do not cease once the physical infrastructure has been put into place. There are several ongoing postconstruction costs associated with technical support, teacher inservicing, and hardware and software upgrading and maintenance. Such initiatives also rely on momentum. By the late 1990s, wiring initiatives that began in earnest in the mid-1990s were losing some of their federal funding support (Mendels, 1998a, 1998b). Nevertheless, the impetus to modernize both elementary and secondary schools remains strong even as school districts increasingly turn to the private sector to help support their technological infrastructure programs.

In addition to outside funding support, there are also choices to be made concerning the organization of computer workstations. Space is always at a premium in classrooms and introducing even just a few computers places new demands on the infrastructure, routine, and layout of a learning space. How computers are to be integrated into a classroom largely depends on the ways in which the technology is to be used in the everyday curriculum. If computers are to be taught as a separate subject, a laboratory model might best be adopted. Classes can book or be regularly rotated through a designated computer lab in a school. This approach helps to formalize the schoolwide use of a limited number of computers, but it doesn't do much to effectively integrate computers into the everyday curriculum.

A more integrated approach situates one or more computer workstations in each classroom of a school. Ideally, each workstation boasts a number of amenities for printing documents, surfing the Web, scanning pictures, building databases, composing music, recording narration, creating multimedia and video presentations, and so forth. Within this scenario, computers are defined less as workstations and more as project studios that can assist students in completing various production-related tasks. When integrated into a whole language curriculum, the computer likely serves as the final destination for a student who is ready to publish the final version of a story. Within such a scenario, it is important to build strong curricular links between computer project stations and non–computer-related learning tasks so that real-world learning opportunities are not lost. A system also needs to be put in place to fairly manage each student's access to and use of the computer workstation(s) in a classroom.

HEALTHY SCHOOLS

The above overview of selected trends and initiatives in contemporary school design would seem to indicate that, despite the current budgetary crunch, all is well with school buildings across the United States. School districts are responding constructively to declining budgets with community use plans, accessibility initiatives, specialty schools, multipurpose spaces, energy efficiencies, technologically savvy designs, and other forward-thinking initiatives. Innovative design plans for schools are receiving the praise they deserve at school design Web sites such as www.designshare.com and www.edfacilities.org.

While it is true that significant attention is now being paid to the design of new schools, there has also been a dawning awareness among U.S. school administrators, elected officials, and the public at large that the same cannot be said of existing school buildings, many of which are currently plagued by poor maintenance and upkeep. (Schools elsewhere in the world, including Canada and Britain, would not appear to be immune from similar problems [Dudek, 2000a; Toronto Star, 1998]). Throughout the last decade and a half, a series of reports prepared by the Education Writers Association (1989), the National Governors Association (1991), the American Association of School Administrators (1991), and the U.S. General Accounting Office (1997) have raised serious questions about the deteriorating physical condition of American schools (Lewis et al., 2001).

Using data gathered in self-reports from a sample of school officials across the country, the U.S. General Accounting Office estimated in 1997 that well over $100 billion would be needed to bring existing schools into good overall condition and at least one third of U.S. schools would need extensive repair or replacement. Many K–12 schools are suffering from incidences of peeling paint, crumbling plaster, leaky roofs, poor lighting, inadequate ventilation, and inoperative heating and cooling systems, among other problems (Frazier, 1993; Perkins, 2001). About 60% of schools have at least one major infrastructure problem and over 40% of schools report at least one unsatisfactory environmental condition (Lyons, 2002; U.S. General Accounting Office, 1997). The above reports conclude that only a massive financial investment in rebuilding the physical infrastructure of the nation's schools will provide an adequate long-term solution to the current crisis.

The reasons for the above problems are varied. Just under half of the schools in the United States today were constructed between 1950 and 1970, a period of rapid growth, and many were not built to last. These older schools tended to rely on cheaper building materials and shortsighted plans that do not meet current safety standards:

> Too often, 1950s schools were built too cheaply for true economy, since yearly maintenance and operation costs were not properly calculated. Lightweight structures, poorly insulated roofs and walls, cheap hardware, poor-quality lighting, minimal ventilation systems, and endlessly repeated standardized plans and elevations characterized many schools. (Brubaker, 1998, p. 15)

Next, there is the issue of overcrowding. Schools with more than 600 students are more likely to be overcrowded than schools with lower enrollments (National Center for Education Statistics [NCES], 2001). (Contrast this with the growing phenomenon of megasized secondary schools, which purposefully house student populations exceeding 2,000 or even 5,000.) Schools with a large percentage of minority students are more likely to report overcrowding. Purchase requisitions for portable classrooms (of questionable environmental health and disconnected from the main school building) are at an all-time high (Lyons, 2002). Although school districts are responsible for the upkeep of school buildings, education is a state responsibility and the necessary state funds needed to upgrade or expand a school district's educational facilities are not always forthcoming (Frazier, 1993). As well, many school districts have shortsighted maintenance and upgrading policies related to current budgetary realities that pit the merits of costly school maintenance plans against the allocation of funds for academic programs and other (more visible) community infrastructure needs. Lisa Walker (1992) summarizes the situation in this way:

> Declining populations in older communities and urban areas, and a loss of jobs and tax base have made it hard for most communities to invest the funds needed. Unfortunately, existing school buildings are with us for too long and are too unexciting for most of that cycle to receive good care and attention from public policymakers. If you can't cut a ribbon or win an award for it in this year, there are few arguments for building a budget around it. And for those communities experiencing a declining tax base, funds for new construction have been nonexistent. (p. 10)

The school infrastructure challenge is so great that it has garnered presidential attention. In responding to the crisis, President Clinton, in a speech in November 1996, announced a federal initiative to rebuild the threatened infrastructure of the nation's public schools through a massive reinvestment of federal resources in school upgrading programs. The president characterized the challenge in these terms:

> The [General Accounting Office] report shows that our nation's schools are increasingly rundown, overcrowded and technologically ill-equipped. Too many school buildings and classrooms are literally a shambles. According to the report, one-third of our schools need major repair or outright replacement; 60 percent need work on major building features—a sagging roof, a cracked foundation; 46 percent lack even the basic electrical wiring to support computers, modems, and modern communications technology. These problems are found all across America, in cities and suburbs.

Throughout its second mandate (1996–2000), the Clinton administration launched a series of public relations efforts aimed at substantially increasing the funds allotted by the federal government for the physical upgrading of schools, but such calls generally fell on deaf ears in the new Republican-controlled Congress, which instead promoted competing priorities for education over the $1.2 billion it appropriated for the emergency repair and renovation of impoverished and rural schools.

Federal and state initiatives to improve the maintenance and upkeep of educational facilities could, over time, bring American schools up to spec in terms of their basic foundations (and indeed, U.S. school construction expenditures have risen by 65% between 1994 and 1999 [NCES, 2002]), but there are also a number of other health and safety factors that are of relevance to the design of schools today. The following discussion briefly underscores the importance of three such factors: concerns for the physical safety of students and staff, the elimination of harmful contaminants from schools, and the call for ergonomically designed furniture.

Physical Safety

> The Dallas public school system recently opened Townview Magnet Center, a high school occupying three city blocks and 375,000 square feet under a single roof. Built to accommodate 2,200 students, the school cost $41 million. Of that amount, approximately $3.5 million was spent on security. The school boasts 37 surveillance cameras, six metal detectors, an intruder-resistant fence that is eight feet high, catwalks in the cafeterias to facilitate student supervision, floodlights that illuminate the school at night . . . and a security staff of five full-time police officers. (Duke, 1998, p. 690)

In violent and impoverished communities across North America, schools have historically been viewed as refuges to which children could escape the danger and uncertainty that might otherwise engulf their lives. Yet, in recent years, it has become readily apparent, particularly in highly congested urban neighborhoods, that a school is not immune to the community violence that occurs outside its walls. Sharp increases in incidences of guns and knives being brought to school by students and highly publicized cases of assault and murder on school property—small towns such as Columbine, Jonesboro, and Stockton are now infamous—have prompted school districts to search for ways of combating the *seemingly* (NCES, 2001) increasing streak of violence in schools. In addition, homeland security fears have prompted yet another wave of school security concerns ("Schools Mull" 2003). Some of these reforms involve changes to the physical infrastructure of school buildings, including the installation of metal detectors, entry check points, and physical barriers that control the flow of traffic through a school.

Although no plan can absolutely guarantee the safety of students and staff, there are a number of helpful design measures that can be adopted to reduce the likelihood of violence. Some schools have implemented a "crime prevention through environmental design plan" (Crowe, 1991, p. 81) that begins with a safety audit of a school's interior and exterior spaces. This audit comprises, in part, a use analysis of all of the spaces within a school, focused particularly on those spaces which are commonly identified as problem areas (e.g., hallways, bathrooms, locker rooms, school grounds, and parking lots) because of their isolated or crowded nature. In conducting a safety audit, the Center for the Prevention of School Violence (1997) suggests that attention:

> be focused upon the school's physical features, layout, and policies and procedures which are in place to handle daily activities as well as problems that may arise. The buildings and grounds of the school should be assessed. Access to the school should be reviewed, and policies, procedures, and techno-

> logical devices, such as alarms and surveillance cameras, should be consid-
> ered to minimize intrusions from outsiders. . . . Determining if a school is
> secure begins by making sure that the above considerations are evidenced
> in the safe school plan and the school's implementation of the plan. . . .
> [As well] perceptions of safety and feelings about safety reveal important
> information about a school's climate. Do students feel safe at school? Do
> teachers? Do parents perceive that the school is safe? . . . Answers to these
> questions initially provide baseline indicators for security, and over time
> the number of occurrences of these types of activities [and perceptions]
> provide measures of how secure a school is. (p. 1)

Once problem spaces are identified, appropriate steps can be taken to reduce the risk of potential conflict or victimization. A plan that combines a
number of physical design initiatives (e.g., the installation of lighting,
monitoring equipment, and/or physical barriers) with new programmatic
and policy reforms can be implemented.

As with other secondary schools across the United States, Belen High
School, near Albuquerque, New Mexico, has coupled changes to the physical design of the school with programmatic reforms that aim to keep students and staff safe (Lockridge, 1998). Working with experts from a nearby
security firm, the staff of this school adopted a three-pronged security plan
which incorporates high-tech, low-tech, and no-tech initiatives. From a
programmatic perspective, teachers keep a high profile in the hallways in
order to monitor the flow of student traffic between classes. Each hall
monitor is equipped with a walkie-talkie that can be used to summon help
immediately. Second, a strict parent pickup policy is enforced at the school
and every visitor to the school must first pass through an entry checkpoint.
Physical changes to the building include doors that are locked on the outside to protect the school from intruders, as well as the installation of a
number of motion detectors and video cameras that monitor key areas,
including the "penalty box" for disruptive students and the parking lot.
Transparent covers have been installed over the school's fire alarms to
reduce incidences of false alarms. To prevent the concealment of drugs
and weapons, all lockers have been bolted shut and are no longer used.
Students now carry their belongings within the school. According to the
principal, students originally did not buy into the security measures but,
over time, these measures have garnered increasing support from both students and staff and students now report that they feel safer.

Classroom Contaminants

> Over the past forty or fifty years, exposure to indoor air pollutants has in-
> creased due to a variety of factors, including the construction of more tightly

sealed buildings, reduced ventilation rates to save energy, the use of synthetic building materials, furnishings, and chemically-formulated personal care products, pesticides, and housekeeping supplies. In addition, our activities and decisions, such as delaying maintenance to "save" money, can lead to problems. . . . Indoor air problems can be subtle and do not always produce easily recognized impacts on health, well-being, or the physical plant. Children are especially susceptible to air pollution. . . . Air quality in schools is of particular concern. (U.S. Environmental Protection Agency, 1996, p. 3)

It is a sad truth that the issue of contaminants is featured so prominently in the history of school design in North America. Whereas physical hazards associated with poor maintenance and public safety are readily identified, invisible dangers such as poor air and water quality, inadequate ventilation, and chemical contaminants, such as poorly stored cleaning materials, can remain undiagnosed in a school for years. Historically, schools have been constructed with little or no attention to the impact that biological and chemical agents will have on the quality of indoor environments. Even less attention has been paid to the chemicals sprayed on the grassy play areas outside of the school.

Young children, in particular, are at greater risk than adults for exposure to such chemicals due to their lower body weight, faster breathing patterns and metabolisms, and more frequent hand-to-mouth contact. In addition, children tend to play on the floor and lawn surfaces where chemicals are often applied (U.S. General Accounting Office, 1999).

Only in recent years, due to public and scientific scrutiny, has the problem of contaminants in schools risen to the fore as a long overdue public health concern. In addition to the well-publicized health risks, exposure to poor indoor air quality can negatively impact on student learning, achievement, and teacher productivity:

Most alarming is the effect of poor indoor air quality on school-age children. Research indicates that the quality of air inside public school facilities may significantly affect students' ability to concentrate. The evidence suggest that youth, especially those under ten years of age, are more vulnerable than adults to the types of contaminants (asbestos, radon, and formaldehyde) found in some school facilities. . . . It is unreasonable to expect positive results from students, teachers, and principals who daily work in an adverse environment. (Frazier, 1993, p. 2)

Without a doubt, the most notorious and pervasive contaminant in schools is asbestos. Due to its excellent thermal properties—it is fireproof and a good heat insulator—asbestos has been a staple of building construction since the 1950s (Castaldi, 1987). In the postwar period, walls and ceilings in newly constructed schools were routinely built using a concrete mixture containing asbestos. So, too, due to its insulation and sound-proofing qualities, asbestos was sprayed on classroom ceilings and plastered around boilers and steam pipes. In its solid form, asbestos is relatively harmless, but once it becomes airborne—after peeling off walls, ceilings, and steam pipes over time—it functions as a cancer-causing agent, a risk to all who inhabit a school.

In an effort to lower concentrations of asbestos and other air pollutants in schools, the U.S. Environmental Protection Agency (1996) recommended the following control strategies:

- *Source Management*: Removal or substitution of the offending material. This is the most effective strategy short of preventing pollutants from entering the environment in the first place.
- *Air Cleaning*: Filtration of offending materials as they move through ventilation equipment before being released into the air.
- *Ventilation*: Dilution of contaminated air with cleaner (outdoor) air. Lowers the concentration of offending materials in the air.
- *Exposure Control*: Relocation of offending materials to uninhabited storage locations. Rescheduling of contaminating practices (e.g., floor waxing) to off-peak hours of school use.

Beyond the above initiatives, school districts can take a number of other practical steps aimed at reducing the health risks associated with working in and attending school (Kowalski, 1989). Where absent, school district policy guidelines for contaminants can be drawn up and regularly updated. School communities can conduct regular environmental and air-quality audits in order to ensure that they are in compliance with local air-standard regulations. Effective hygiene procedures can be put into practice by teachers, students, and custodial staff. Animal, plant, and microbiology specimens, as well as chemical agents used in school science labs, art departments, and industrial shops, can be stored securely in well-ventilated locations. Where air-quality problems are found, the necessary steps needed to rectify the situation can be taken immediately, irrespective of cost, in order to avoid liability and ensure the long-term health of students and staff.

Ergonomic Furniture

While visiting a computer lab with my daughter and her grade two class, I watched while the children got a crash course in the use of various software programs. Although the chairs swiveled and were adjustable, they had clearly been made for adult bodies. . . . Missing from the lesson was any guidance on correct hand and body posture at the keyboard. No one mentioned that the chairs were adjustable and could be made more comfortable for children of different sizes. . . . The equipment was completely out of proportion for virtually the entire group of seven-year-olds. Consequently, all of these children spent the morning with their heads tilted upwards at the screen in a posture designed to put strain on the spine and give them sore necks. (Armstrong & Casement, 1998, p. 154)

It was noted earlier that the architects of Crow Island School paid close attention to both the macro- and micro-level issues of school design. In an unusual move, the architects themselves designed the child-scaled furniture for the school, ensuring that it was both functional and aesthetically congruent with the larger design patterns that were at work in the school as a whole. Today, the decision to use custom-designed, rather than prefabricated, furniture remains the exception rather than the rule. Most schools purchase generic furniture which is then used for multiple purposes and age groups. (One teacher told me that he didn't so much mind the drab green or orange chairs that are in common use throughout North American schools, but he certainly dreaded being assigned a classroom each fall that had a combination of the two.) Yet there is a growing awareness of the need to ensure that the design of tables, chairs, and other furniture conform to ergonomically acceptable standards and that the specific purposes to which school furniture is put is both age- and use-appropriate (Perkins, 2001).

The science of ergonomics has emerged from relative obscurity in the early decades of the 20th century to highlight one of the most important technology-related health issues of the early 21st century. As increasing numbers of adults spend more and more time in front of computers in offices and other workplace environments, there has emerged a pressing concern for the rising number of office workers who are afflicted with carpal tunnel syndrome, otherwise known as repetitive stress injury. And while it is the practical implications of ergonomics to the workplace that have received the most attention, there are also important lessons for schools. Consider, for example, the redeployment of traditional desks and other furniture to serve as computer tables in schools (Buck, 1994). Many schools spend thousands or even tens of thousands of dollars annually to equip their computer labs and classrooms with the latest computer hardware and software, but the tables upon which this equipment sits are often an afterthought. Although computers are today used by both younger and older children for ever-increasing amounts of time each year, the desks upon which this equipment is placed are often of fixed height, putting the computer keyboard, mouse, and monitor at an awkward angle for those children who are too short or too tall to work comfortably with the computer for extended periods of time (see Figure 3.6). Moreover, the chairs that students sit on are unlikely to be adjustable in height. With young children spending increasing amounts of time at the computer, advocates of ergonomic furniture argue that there is an urgent need to resurrect a concern for the design of school furniture, to renew our commitment to making child-scaled furniture that is both ergonomic and age- and use-appropriate.

THE PHILOSOPHY OF SCHOOL DESIGN

If the above discussion is any indication, there would seem to be two opposing sets of forces at work in American schools today—first, an innovative and cost-efficient design strategy for new schools and, second, from a

FIGURE 3.6. School districts spend many thousands of dollars on computers each year, but the ergonomics of the furniture that houses these computers is very often an afterthought.

somewhat more cynical point of view, an inattentive and patchwork-based upgrading scheme for many older schools. The first path is progressive, the second regressive. Yet both are united in a common guiding principle— that cost efficiency, driven by current budgetary realities, should be a primary criterion upon which school design and improvement plans are made.

Yet should budgetary reality be the most important factor taken into account in designing schools? A number of school design advocates (e.g., Black, 2001; Duke, 1998; Sanoff, 1994) would beg to differ. They argue that there are other, more or equally important, considerations with demonstrable links to student achievement, teacher productivity, school morale, and social adjustment, that also need to be factored into school construction plans. In supporting such a view, this chapter closes by briefly reviewing the arguments of two key school design advocates.

C. William Brubaker

C. William Brubaker is a principal at the Perkins & Will architectural firm, the designers of the historic Crow Island School discussed earlier in this chapter. A preeminent architect of school buildings throughout the United States, Brubaker has three times been given the Honor Award of the American Institute of Architects. Reflecting on over 30 years of school design experience, Brubaker's architectural philosophy (1998) aims to balance a forward-looking vision for the future with a sensitivity to the practical realities of building schools.

Schools should be innovative. School designers should take risks in planning the designs of schools. Instead of following a "cookie-cutter" approach, school planners should recognize the role they can play in forging new traditions in educational architecture and pedagogy. Historically innovative design plans for schools, such as flexible and adaptable spaces, specialized labs, broadbased technology shops, and the community school concept are now commonplace, but they are only here now because of the pioneering efforts of early school planners:

> When an architecture for education innovation catches on, it can spread and change the way we plan, design, and use school buildings and the equipment schoolhouses contain. To discourage innovation would be to signal that experimentation and changes in school design are not welcome; stagnation (motionless, dull, inactive, stale conditions) then would dominate. (p. 37)

Schools should be regionally congruent. Just as the curriculum of a school should be responsive to the local community context, so too should the design of a school reflect the natural and cultural uniqueness of the larger region or locale in which it is situated. Local history, a region's geographical features, cultural makeup, primary industries, and so on, should all be taken into consideration during the early planning stages. By way of example, Brubaker cites the unique architectural heritage of aboriginal and Hispanic cultures as perfect inspirations for the form, material makeup, and decor of New Mexico public schools. By demonstrating a congruency between design and culture, school planners honor the traditions of the surrounding community.

Schools should be adaptable. Schools that are built today will be used well into the 21st century, possibly even into the 22nd century, and we cannot know the varying educational philosophies that will come into play as societal and technological conditions change. Therefore, the same all-important first principles of school design in the late 20th century—flexibility and adaptability—need to continue to guide school construction. Schools need to incorporate flexible learning spaces with movable walls, folding partitions, and lightweight furniture that can be quickly redeployed to accommodate smaller or larger class sizes, teacher work areas, and specialized labs and media/resource centers.

Schools should be preserved. As the school infrastructure crisis deepens, educational planners need to enter into a critical discussion on just what constitutes a school worth preserving. During the 1950s and 1960s, many older schools—some well worth preserving—were demolished in favor of new schools that employed modern facility designs. Some of these 1950s schools are today in dire need of repair and decisions need to be made concerning which schools are worth salvaging and which are not. For such schools, the severity of the physical infrastructure problems, the financial resources needed to fix these problems, demographic trends in the local community, and other factors need to be taken into consideration. Since the school infrastructure challenge is a national one and any collective decisions that are reached could remake the landscape of education throughout the United States, school designers need to stake out a role in the school infrastructure debate.

William Bradley

The mission of the Thomas Jefferson Center for Educational Design is to highlight the role of the built environment in improving the quality of education in K–12 schools (Duke, 1998). Associates at the center include representatives from the fields of architecture, business, education, engineering, sociology, and technology. As an instructor at the center, William Bradley argues that there is a direct relationship between effective school design and quality education. In his quest to seek out exemplary models of educational facility planning, Bradley (1998) highlights the following principles of effective school design.

Schools should be exemplary. Educational facilities should model the values and ideals that educators want children to learn. For example, schools should be welcome to all, rather than be accessible to able-bodied people alone. Technological amenities should be integrated into facility design plans from the beginning of the school design process rather than implemented as an afterthought. Instead of moving to a dedicated computer lab for instruction, computers should instead be incorporated into the design of each classroom so that the physical placement of computers in classrooms reinforces the pedagogical integration of technology into every facet of the curriculum. From an ecological perspective, schools should emulate the environmental design choices that students will need to make as adults by incorporating environmentally friendly energy use strategies.

Schools should direct. Visual cues should be incorporated into the design of educational facilities so that schools can take advantage of the "fundamentals of architectural design to relay cues to a building's users subtly, naturally, and effectively" (Bradley, 1998, p. 5). Bradley emphasizes that this is not an invitation to post more signs. On the contrary, the basic form and function of the school building itself should incorporate physical cues that capture the mood of the school, help navigate visitors, and encourage certain behaviors over others (e.g., walking over running).

Schools should evoke a spirit of place. At the beginning of this chapter, the typical school was characterized as "a brick box with holes for windows in a style that can only be described as neutered" (Graves, 1993, p. 25). Not surprisingly, Bradley argues against this uniform, prison-like design for schools and instead calls for the place-conscious school, an educational facility that reflects through its design the scale, culture, and pace of the surrounding community:

> Our schools have taken on a distinctly institutional look. Too often in our rush to expedite design we have reduced educational programs to their lowest common denominator . . . uniform spaces [that] lack character and fail to provide a meaningful context for learning. . . . [Schools should] be places in which students gain a sense of identity. . . . Schools should reference the settings in which they are built. (1998, p. 7)

Schools should teach. The design of schools should foster in students an appreciation for their surroundings, including both the natural and built environments. The environment of the school should be thought of as a three-dimensional textbook for learning. Architectural education programs that emphasize the themes of balance, order, symmetry, pattern, rhythm, form, space, and scale should be taught to children by way of reference to the school itself and the surrounding community.

At the root of Bradley's prescription for school design is an ideological vantage point that celebrates the school as a community of learners. From this holistic perspective, many of the considerations noted above may also extend to the design of the classroom itself. The next chapter explores selected examples of classroom design and the ideological orientations that connect the organization of classroom space to the philosophy of education, developmental psychology, instructional methodology, and curriculum.

Chapter 4

VISIONS OF DYNAMIC SPACE

What would happen if classrooms weren't square "just because"? How much better could our schools be if we taught students in learning environments that contributed to, rather than distracted from, the educational program? What would happen if we based our designs on the philosophy of the school and the curriculum being taught?
—William Bradley (1998, p. 12)

Messages are sent by the way the classroom is laid out, whether we, as teachers, are conscious of these messages or not.
—Paul Theobald (1997, p. 140)

One of the most important decisions that new teachers make in preparing for their first year of teaching pertains to how the classroom itself will embody and promote their teaching philosophy and help to manage student behavior. An initial concern is the arrangement of the students' desks. Will my classroom promote collaborative learning or a direct instruction approach to teaching? In the case of the former, desks are perhaps best arranged in groups. In the case of the latter, desks might better be organized into rows. Next, there is the issue of meeting areas and other open spaces for student collaboration. Will my classroom function as a community of learners or emphasize the individual achievement of each student working on one's own? Collaborative work spaces can help to promote a cooperative learning ethic among students, but such communal areas may not always be appropriate if one instead wishes to promote a competitive ethic that places a premium on individual achievement.

The choices that teachers make in organizing the layout of their classrooms both promote and constrain the kinds of learning that occur in a classroom. Teachers who populate their classrooms with various arts and crafts supplies, manipulatives, and other materials for students to work with are actively promoting a participatory, dynamic learning environment, but the opportunities for transmitting information in an explicit, systematic way are potentially reduced. On the other hand, teachers who

77

adopt a direct instruction approach to teaching are likely to forgo opportunities for decentralized, participatory learning in favor of an explicit, systematic teaching approach.

Yet beyond all of the practical trade-offs of organizing a classroom in this way or that are the very real ideological differences that are impressed upon new teachers by public sentiment, teacher education faculties, mentor teachers, boards of education, school administrators, colleagues, students, and parents. So, too, by the time they have graduated, many beginning teachers have formed their own personal vision of what they would like their classroom to look like, a classroom ideal that is closely connected to their teaching philosophy and professional goals.

This chapter addresses the connection between ideology and place in education by highlighting the relationship between the philosophy of education and school and classroom design. The chapter summarizes and (where relevant) critiques four educational movements, each of which argues for a particular vision of place in education. These movements are: Montessori, Waldorf, open education, and school ground naturalization. Drawing from the underlying tenets of these movements, a concluding section highlights a number of conceptual dichotomies that further frame the relationship between educational ideology and the construction of place in schools.

With the exception of the Waldorf schools, each of the above approaches to the organization of classroom space arises in sharp contrast to the traditional layout of classrooms into rows of desks (see Figure 4.1). (Waldorf and traditional approaches can be contrasted in other ways.) Despite going out of fashion in educational academia in recent years, the traditional arrangement of desks into rows is still in evidence in many, if not most, classrooms today and should not be discounted. The unique advantages that such a layout boasts over the more complex alternative layouts explored in this chapter may help to explain its longevity. By having students face the same direction and sit apart from one another, the challenges of surveillance and discipline are managed more easily. So, too, the arrangement of desks into cells makes both for clearer pathways in and around each student's desk and metaphorically supports the notion of the individual as a discrete learning unit. Most importantly, the historic arrangement of desks into rows directly supports a traditional instructional approach, in which teaching essentially involves the one-way transmission of content from teacher-as-lecturer to large numbers of students. Within such an approach, students are judged to be the receptive recipients of factual information which is systematically organized and presented by the teacher. Information is explicit, rather than contextual; objective rather than personal; and rarely open to dispute—hence there is no need

FIGURE 4.1. The traditional classroom layout boasts an efficient seating plan that values quiet seatwork. Tennis balls on the legs of each student's chair minimize squeaking.

for personal reflection or discussion. Instruction follows a linear flow and is carefully organized by the teacher in advance of the lesson. The effective organization and presentation of information is the hallmark of successful teaching within this tradition.

As noteworthy alternatives to the direct instruction tradition, my choice of the Montessori, Waldorf, open, and naturalization movements is not arbitrary. Each showcases a different (albeit innovative) direction for educational reform and the organization of learning spaces. The Montessori movement puts forward a precisely structured and intellectually grounded view of classroom space. The Waldorf movement counters this sentiment with an aesthetically grounded milieu. The open and naturalization movements each aim to open up the learning environment by breaking down the barriers to learning and targeting nontraditional settings, respectively. Each of these four movements takes the notion of learning settings very seriously. Indeed, in sharp contrast to most other educational movements, the idea of place is integral to a full understanding of each philosophy. Moreover, the underpinnings of each philosophy are representative of competing agendas for school reform—their underlying tenets are not reducible to each other. Despite having made recent inroads into public education, two of the traditions (Montessori and Waldorf) are fundamentally private school alternatives. One tradition (open plan education) has gone out of fashion, while another (school ground naturalization) is only now emerging as a grassroots initiative around the world.

THE PREPARED ENVIRONMENT

> When I first pointed out the great value of an environment specially adapted . . . to the needs of little children, this idea aroused great interest in architects, artists, and psychologists, some of whom collaborated with me to settle the ideal size and height of the rooms, and the decorations desirable in a school where concentration was to be favored. Such a building was more than protective and might almost be called "psychological." Yet its value did not depend entirely on dimensions and coloring—which are not enough in themselves—but it depended on the things provided for the children's use, for the child needs tangible things on which to focus his attention. Yet these things . . . were not decided arbitrarily, but only as a result of prolonged experimentation with children themselves. (Montessori, 1995, pp. 222–223)

Maria Montessori's (1870–1952) notion of the *prepared environment* may be the most explicit example of the intersection of philosophy and place in K–12 education. The founder of one of the most widespread independent school movements in the world, Montessori originally trained in Italy as a medical doctor before gaining a sound reputation and international following for her work with developmentally challenged and nonhandicapped preschool children. Montessori developed a theory of child development and a method of instruction that extends in large measure from her clinical and empirically disciplined study of the child in a self-directed learning environment. Just what Montessori meant by "self-direction" goes a long way in distinguishing this tradition from other alternatives in education.

Montessori (1995) posited the notion of the *absorbent mind* as a way of contrasting the young child's relationship to the world with that of the older child and adult. Only with a mature faculty of mind, argued Montessori, does a person know the world through conscious reasoning and abstract conceptualization. Young children, however, are absorbed in the concrete reality of their world. From birth to age 6, the child builds up one's mind and senses through the absorption of the environment—first,

at the level of the unconscious; and later, through the willful manipula-
tion of concrete materials in a structured learning environment.

Impressions from the world not only penetrate the young child's mind;
they also form it. The basic mental faculties that will support all subsequent learning are formed during this early sensitive period. Through instinctive (birth to age 3) and willful (age 3 to 6) interactions with the world,
or more pointedly, actions *on* the world, the child develops a formative
cosmology of the world and begins the long process of placing herself in
relationship to it.

The most striking example of learning by absorption is that of language acquisition, the universal process by which children all around the
world subconsciously and seemingly without effort pick up their native
tongue. Children everywhere learn the subtleties of language, including
its grammar, syntax, and semiotics, in direct and intimate relationship with
the world. Montessori argued that many of the same learning principles
that hold true for language acquisition also hold true for cognitive development in the early years of a child's life.

First, cognitive learning is an individual exercise and cannot be taught.
It is the young child's self-regulated interactions with the world that spurs
on cognitive development, not the explicit lessons given by a parent or
teacher, nor a child's social interactions with her peers. Second, young children delight in repetitive activity that subconsciously impresses and reinforces basic physical, spatial, and mental concepts on the mind. Throughout
early childhood, independence and self-confidence are strengthened
through the child's achievements in these areas. Finally, all cognitive learning throughout this period occurs through the reciprocal interaction of environment, motor skills, and mind. In short, children learn by doing.

Montessori posited the notion of the prepared environment (see Figure 4.2) as a constructed and ordered learning space, set apart from that
of older children and adults, where young children could go to further their
learning through repetitive and individualized hands-on exercises that
promote cognitive growth:

> The structured environment for learning involves the use of a wide range of
> didactic apparatus. . . . Children thrive on learning when they choose those
> materials which seem to fulfill a specific need in them. The focus of the
> Montessori curriculum is on mastery of one's self and environment. . . .
> Repetition is necessary for the child to refine his senses, perfect his skills,
> and build up competency and knowledge. . . . The child revels in repeating
> those things which he knows best and does well. (Hainstock, 1986, p. 68)

When you first walk into a Montessori preschool, the first thing you
are likely to notice is the orderliness of the classroom. Manipulative

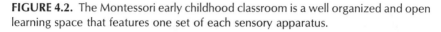

FIGURE 4.2. The Montessori early childhood classroom is a well organized and open learning space that features one set of each sensory apparatus.

materials are carefully laid out along the walls and easily accessible to the children. Child-sized tables where two or three children can work independently, but alongside one another, are placed throughout the room. The classroom is brightly colored, child-scaled, and clean. Montessori also wanted the classroom to be beautiful (Lillard, 1973, p. 59), but most of all she wanted it to be functional. The functional congruence of the environment with the cognitive developmental needs of children is of paramount importance and outweighs any "purely aesthetic considerations" (Standing, 1984, p. 268).

At its core, the Montessori method is straightforward. It is this straightforwardness that structures in advance the roles and routines of both child and teacher. Upon arrival, the young child goes to a shelf to choose a didactic material with which to work. She takes her chosen manipulative to a desk or floor space and puts it to repeated use for as long as she wishes, but in the exact way she has been instructed. At her discretion, she returns the material to its storage location and chooses another material with which to work. Meanwhile, the teacher carefully monitors each child's progress, models appropriate sharing and courteous behavior, handles discipline situations as they arise, prepares the Montessori apparatus and, when developmentally appropriate, introduces one or more children to the proper usage of a new manipulative.

It is important to note that the description given above conforms to what might be described as the prepared environment proper. There is a whole other dimension to the Montessori preschool experience which incorporates practical life exercises, gardening, and playhouse-like settings for role-modeling cultural activities. So, too, in recent years, some Montessori schools have begun to compliment the conventional Montessori method described above with group activities that involve music, drama, and other social pursuits. Nevertheless, it is the prepared environment proper which forms the basis of all Montessori preschool programs, both historically and at present.

The foremost aim of the prepared environment is to render the child autonomous and independent of the adult. Effective learning is the result of the child's focused interactions with the Montessori materials, rather than the teacher's mediation of that interaction (see Figure 4.3). Teacher intervention (when the materials are being used correctly) is seen as an obstacle to growth and the child's striving toward independence, rather than a contribution to it. The same holds true for the child's peers. Cognitive learning is judged to be a largely asocial activity in early childhood. It is reducible to the quality of a young child's focused interactions with the manipulatives that make up the Montessori curriculum.

Not surprisingly, there are explicit rules that determine the usage of space and materials in a Montessori classroom. For example, children are taught to share and engage in courteous and orderly behavior when moving materials to and from their shelf space:

> Within the Montessori classroom there is only one set of didactic materials, unlike schools where there might be several sets of the same kind of toy. The didactic materials are arranged similarly in all Montessori schools. . . . According to Montessori, finding things in their proper places and putting them back again satisfies the child's need for order. . . . A child may take a didactic material from the place where it is stored and when the child has finished using it, the material must be put back in its place and in the same condition it was found. (DeJesus, 1987, pp. 16, 27–28)

While children are free to change exercises as they wish and move about the classroom for the purpose of exchanging manipulatives, they are not free to use the Montessori materials in any way they see fit. This

FIGURE 4.3. Montessori valued children's independence from peer and teacher intervention. The Montessori materials are designed to be self-correcting.

is because each manipulative has been carefully crafted and perfected, often over the course of several years, to serve a particular purpose and impress and/or reinforce a specific concept on the child's mind.

Montessori also chose the materials she did because of the satisfaction and inner peace children exhibited as they took ownership of the materials and used them to build up their minds:

> The sensorial materials are each designed to convey an abstract idea in concrete form. . . . A tower of cubes demonstrates volume and size; a series of rods, the concept of length. . . . [Where] feasible the sensorial materials are composed of sets of ten objects, giving the children an indirect exposure to the basis of the decimal system. . . . The exactness of these materials appeals to the human tendency for precision and gives the children an experience of the realities upon which human technology is based. (Lillard, 1996, pp. 35–36)

The combination of a well-thought-out developmental vision and overtly structured learning environment has made the Montessori tradition something of an enigma in educational circles. On the one hand, there is a strong congruency between the prepared environment and Montessori's carefully articulated cognitive developmental theory that endears the Montessori method to the progressive and holistic education movements with which it is commonly associated. Montessori's developmental theory has much in common with Piaget's theory of cognitive development, which itself has been applied to modern progressive education. (Unlike Montessori, however, Piaget did not see a role for formal education in promoting a young child's early cognitive growth.) Likewise, the more esoteric elements of the Montessori tradition (e.g., her Christian mysticism and conception of the child as a *spiritual embryo*) are congruent with the holistic focus on the spiritual development of the child. Yet the issue of freedom, a tenuous notion in both progressive and holistic education (Hutchison, 1998), arises as a sore point for some observers of the Montessori system who have at times criticized what they see as the rigid and anti-social nature of the prepared environment proper (e.g., Polakow, 1992). Montessori counters this sentiment with the following:

> The children in our schools are free, but that does not mean there is no organization. Organization, in fact, is necessary, and if the children are to be free to *work*, it must be even more thorough than in the ordinary schools. (1995, p. 244)

In Montessori's view, a child's self-discipline and love of learning (i.e., work) emerge spontaneously. Neither need be imposed from without. She believed that the child identifies in tasks the opportunities to develop one's human potential. The child concentrates and perseveres on tasks for long periods of time (Montessori, 1995) and the child's excitement grows as new discoveries are made about the world (Lillard, 1973).

From the Montessori perspective, a highly structured environment makes sense insofar as it directly provides the cognitive inputs yearned for by the young child during this early sensitive period. What appears to the outside observer as severe restrictions on the use of materials, fantasy play, and child interaction intentionally supports the Montessori belief that cognitive learning, until the age of about 6, is an individual enterprise that demands each child's focused attention as he or she strives toward independence in thought and action.

While children do not interfere or work collaboratively with other children, they *do* observe other (often older) children at work, which in turn inspires them to achieve success in their own work. In a scenario that subtly foreshadows the design philosophy of open-plan schools (which will be discussed later), Montessori illustrates how the open space of the prepared environment encourages younger children to use the work of older children as a model:

> The classroom for those of three to six is not even rigidly separated from that of the children from seven to nine. Thus, children of six can get ideas from the class above. Our dividing walls are only waist-high partitions, and there is always easy access from one classroom to the next. Children are free to pass to and fro between classrooms. . . . There are demarcations but no separations, and all the groups can intercommunicate. Each has its appointed place but it is not isolated: one can always go for an intellectual walk! . . . [A young child of 6] may see another of nine using beads to perform the arithmetical operation of extracting a square root. He may ask him what he is doing . . . and may stay to watch, learning something from it. . . . The child's progress does not depend only on his age, but also on being free to look about him (1995, pp. 227–228)

The Montessori child does not need to look to adults for guidance on using the Montessori materials. Built into most materials is a feedback mechanism (control-for-error) that can often correct a child's use of a material without the need for adult intervention. The structuredness of the prepared environment aims to reduce not only interruptions by other children, but also potentially distracting mediation by the teacher.

There is a form of environmental determinism at work in Montessori preschools which aims to structure children's actions through the purposeful design, placement, and use restrictions assigned to the Montessori materials and individual workspaces. Yet for the prepared environment to function effectively as a surrogate authority for the teacher, it is necessary that the rules governing its use be understood and shared by all. Thus, children's efforts to transform their learning environment through fantasy play or "inappropriate" use of the materials can prove problematic.

In the Montessori preschool classrooms observed by one critic, the young child "did not possess the history making power to influence her interpersonal environment, nor imprint herself upon the landscape, nor transform her spatial surroundings" (Polakow, 1992, p. 99). A flexibly co-structured learning environment was foregone in favor of the promise that young children, working within the context of a highly structured prepared environment, would develop independence, self-confidence, and an array of inner controls through their successful mastery of the Montessori materials. In the eyes of Montessori advocates, young children delight in the focused work they do with the Montessori materials, the results of which not only "free" their minds, but also propel cognitive learning to new levels of understanding.

THE AESTHETIC ENVIRONMENT

The notion of authority as concretized by Montessori's notion of the prepared environment is not echoed by the Waldorf educational philosophy, although Waldorf educators also see a role for authority in childhood education and take seriously the nature of the learning environment. In the Waldorf philosophy, authority is manifested in the strength of the child-teacher relationship, rather than the structuredness of a prepared environment. In contrast to the intellectual milieu of the Montessori early childhood classroom, Rudolf Steiner, the founder of Waldorf education, argued for the primacy of the aesthetic in designing learning environments for children.

Although there is no evidence to suggest that they ever met, Rudolf Steiner (1861–1925) was a contemporary of Montessori's. An eclectic writer and lecturer, Steiner was in touch with people from many walks of life. His contributions to the fields of art, architecture, agriculture, and theology are all well documented. Early in his career, Steiner was a student of Goethe's spiritual science. Steiner embraced and further developed Goethe's ideas on form and color and applied each to sculpture, painting, and architecture. However, it is Steiner's endeavors related to education which have had the most pervasive influence. In 1919, he founded the first Waldorf school (so named for the factory in which it was situated) in Stuttgart, Germany. Today the Waldorf movement numbers several hundred schools in some 20 countries.

Whereas Montessori's theory of development and education was largely rooted in her clinical and empirically disciplined study of the child within the environment of the classroom, Rudolf Steiner's understanding of childhood education (and other phenomena) emerged from a supersensory awareness of a spiritual world well beyond the material physical world which informed much of the scientific thinking of his time. It was Steiner's lifelong aim to bring the spiritual/artistic and materialistic/scientific communities closer together. Indeed, it is this spirit that perhaps best characterizes the basic philosophy of the Waldorf school movement right up to the present time.

The fusion of science and art, intellect and emotion, and materialism and spirit underscores the design considerations at work in many Waldorf schools. From a purely materialistic perspective, a school building is simply bricks and mortar, but to infuse a school facility with an aesthetic, or even spiritual dimension is to build connections between the physical design of the school and the interior lives of the students, teachers, and staff who inhabit it. As Dennis Sharp (1966) writes:

> Steiner's architecture was really open sculpture; huge pieces of sculpture in which people move and have a new sense of being. . . . [It was] an environment above and around which the primary spaces are created to invoke the response of the Spirit in man. With Steiner the interior spaces were all important. . . . They were "soul spaces" in which there was an important distinction between *real space*, which remains external to man, and *soul space* in which spiritual events, interior to man, were realized. (pp. 153–154)

Unlike most other traditions in education, the physical characteristics of a Waldorf school—including its shape, scale, orientation, interior colors, and material makeup—are themselves explicitly connected to the Waldorf curriculum and theory of child development. The twin foci of form and color in particular find expression in both the architectural and pedagogical principles of Waldorf education. Hence form is not only central to the Waldorf curriculum, through form drawing, clay modeling, and other artistic pursuits, but also to the design of the Waldorf school itself.

Ideally, argued Steiner, the architecture of the school will include archetypal transformations in the repetition of common motifs which, in turn, evoke a metamorphosis of form that echoes those similar metamorphoses of growth that characterize the development of the child (Dudek, 2000a). The ideal form evokes an energy similar to those inner growth forces of the budding plant, the maturing butterfly, or the growing child—organic, dynamic, and archetypal (see Figure 4.4).

Likewise, children's experiments with color figure prominently in the Waldorf curriculum and color is itself judged to be related to children's temperaments (Carlgren, 1976). Yet color also has a moody and spiritual quality within the Waldorf philosophy which has design implications for the hue, texture, and lighting of rooms and corridors. Ideally, argue Waldorf educators, the built and natural environments of the outdoors, home, and school will each reflect and complement, through form, color, and other characteristics, the developmental experience of childhood. In short, the physical makeup of home and school are deemed to have a subtle but important influence on the young child's development, her temperament, affective life, and psychic well-being.

Steiner argued that the surrounding environment permeates children's aesthetic and spiritual lives. He projected well into middle childhood a state of being similar to that of Montessori's own early childhood notion of the unconscious absorbent mind. Yet while Montessori concluded that this

FIGURE 4.4. The central focal point of the Toronto Waldorf School spirals high into the sky, architecturally celebrating the developmental forces that propel growth in childhood.

immersive period ends in late infancy, Steiner (1982) posited an extended period of environmental surrogacy which lasts until about age 9:

> The child is not in a position to distinguish clearly between himself and the outside world; even in his feeling life, the feeling of the world and the feeling of his own ego are not clearly distinguished . . . he looks upon what goes on outside him as a continuation of his own being. (p. 81)

Through the subconscious, instinctive imitation of those around him or her and through the unconscious absorption of the environment, the child comes to know the world and further refine the basis of one's personal identity. The child's consciousness "extends beyond the sphere of her little body," wrote A. C. Harwood (1958, pp. 15–16). "In an impersonal, dream-like, or rather sleep-like, way the child's powers of consciousness are living in her environment." To support this child-centered ideal of place, Steiner proposed something akin to Froebel's (1826/1912) original vision of the kindergarten (Dudek, 2000b) as "a garden of children." The interior of a Waldorf school, with its characteristic fleshy and earth-tone wall colors and beautifully designed spaces for music, dance, and handicrafts, would be purposefully crafted to complement the organic character of a natural setting, the aesthetic needs of the child, and the artistic focus of the Waldorf curriculum:

> [In designing the Hartsbrook Waldorf School in Massachusetts] we focused on the curriculum and its appropriate enhancement through architecture and landscape. Our discussion considered such topics as the spiritual and philosophical foundations of the Waldorf education, the learning path of the child, the characteristic qualities of each class year, and how these qualities may be embodied architecturally. We also explored the vernacular architectural impulse, the land, and its history. The relationships of classroom spaces to the immediate sites and distant views were carefully considered, as were the spaces themselves, in terms of form, color, proportion, and detail. (As quoted in Sanoff, 1994, p. 103)

It is perhaps not surprising, given the organic epistemology of the Waldorf philosophy, that many Waldorf school communities favor rural locales over congested urban sites, a privilege not afforded to schools in most other educational traditions. The Hartsbrook Waldorf School, as noted above, employs a farmhouse motif and takes its silo-like form from the common structures to be found in the neighboring New England rural landscape. Studies in organic farming and seasonal festivals further reinforce the local community context. On the other side of the ocean, the Nant-Y-Cwm Steiner School in Britain is not only situated in a natural setting, but also purposefully set off from the surrounding thoroughfares. The long walk from the parking lot to the school aims to effect a transformation in children's moods as they make their way on foot to class each morning:

> Children will have almost certainly traveled by car . . . having had a kaleidoscopic experience [of sight and sound]. . . . The effect of this synthetic experience may be to make them raucous and fractious. They have therefore about a hundred meters of woodland walk, crossing several thresholds to leave that world behind them. First a leaf archway, then a sun-dappled cliff edge above this shining, singing river . . . Then an invitingly gestured, but slightly asymmetrical . . . entrance. Then a blue purple-green corridor, quiet, low, twisting, darker. (Dudek & Day, as quoted in Dudek, 2000a, p. 77)

Other features of the Nant-Y-Cwm Steiner School further endear it to its natural setting. Classrooms and corridors twist and turn to reveal irregularly curved and organic shapes. Walls taper out at their bases to create the impression of a school that is rooted in the earth. The roof is grass covered. Classrooms feature homemade interior lights and nooks and crannies that await children's discovery. The building is paradoxically both innovative and homey at the same time.

A concern for the organic integrity of the Waldorf school as a whole also finds expression in the design of each classroom. First-time visitors to a Waldorf school may be surprised to learn that, despite the Waldorf movement's holistic underpinnings, students, beginning in the first grade, sit in rows and learn their main lessons in a combined teacher-directed and participatory fashion. There is not, in Waldorf schools, the high degree of childhood independence that is found in Montessori preschools. In part, this arrangement conforms to the Waldorf view on child-teacher authority alluded to earlier. Just as the surrounding environment is deemed to permeate children's aesthetic and spiritual lives, so do young children "live through" parents, teachers, and other adult authority figures in their moral lives. Early childhood learning in a Waldorf school is as much about aesthetic, spiritual, and moral development as it is about intellectual development. Children need the authoritative presence of a teacher they can look up to with reverence.

Upon closer examination, the Waldorf grade school classroom is also revealed to be an aesthetically crafted learning space. Poems on chalkboards are beautifully scripted using multicolored chalk. Handicrafts and artifacts that concretize the topics under study adorn the classroom walls. Rather than being copied from books and photos, many of these artifacts are original works. They are specially crafted by the teacher or other adult and always beautifully framed and presented. Yet Rudolf Steiner argued that the primary purpose of elementary education was to draw out from children, through their imaginations, those images that support learning, rather than presenting pictures and photos as a fait accompli. Indeed, one could argue that the most important "places" in Waldorf education exist in each child's imagination. Such places are evoked through the telling of stories, myths, legends, fairy tales, and other narratives, which are then utilized by teachers as the basis for lessons.

In contrast to the brightly colored, even synthetic character of many traditional learning settings, Waldorf classrooms favor an organic aesthetic that draws from and complements the varied textures, hues, and aromas to be found in nature (see Figure 4.5). Early childhood learning environments in Waldorf schools favor nonfinished natural materials over manufactured toys whose functionality is limited by their intricate and specialized design. Children bring their own imaginations to nonfinished objects, which, in turn, preserve for the child the natural integrity, texture, and imperfections of

FIGURE 4.5. In Waldorf classrooms, elemental materials such as wood, clay, and wool subtly reinforce children's identification with nature. This kindergarten classroom also provides direct access to the natural world outside.

the original material. Waldorf educators believe that elemental materials such as wood, stone, clay, sand, and water have an eternal quality that transcends that of mass-produced playthings. Moreover, natural materials work on a subconscious level to reinforce subtly children's identification with nature (Carlgen, 1976). Having natural materials in the classroom does not simply fulfill children's aesthetic needs. These materials also reach far back in time to embrace an age when the natural world provided the overriding context for human activity. With this in mind, the milieu of the Waldorf classroom aims to imbue a strong agrarian, mythic, and eco-dynamic quality that celebrates a continuity between human culture and nature.

On first reading, the Waldorf and Montessori movements would seem to be worlds apart in their view of place in education. Although both philosophies put forward a detailed vision of child development, the pedagogical implications of their respective visions lead to very different prescriptions for the construction of educational spaces, particularly for young children. The Montessori movement favors an intellectual milieu where young children work consciously to build up their minds. The Waldorf movement favors an aesthetic milieu in which a beautifully crafted learning space subconsciously influences the affective development of children, both young and old. Yet despite their differences, the Montessori and Waldorf traditions share at least one element in common. Both movements subscribe to the view that children require a structured and teacher-planned learning environment. This is in sharp contrast to the open philosophy, to which our discussion will now turn, which supports a flexibly structured and coplanned setting for learning.

THE OPEN ENVIRONMENT

Albert Wicker School, erected in New Orleans in 1974, was originally designed as a three-level open plan school that by its supporters' own admission would put 1,000 students in the equivalent of one room. As with many other educational facilities built or renovated during the 1970s, this school embraced a free and open design philosophy which was congruent with the romantic educational sentiments that were in vogue at the time. Beginning in the late 1960s, concurrent with the rise of the humanistic movement in psychology, affective goals in education began to gain prominence, particularly at the elementary level. A renewed focus on the individualized learning needs of children (an initiative that could trace its roots back to the child-centered reforms of the 1920s) led to a greater concern for children's emotional and social development. The traditional definition of schools as sites for the transmission of knowledge was now expanded to include the culture of the classroom—now viewed to be a community—and the importance of the peer group to child socialization. Likewise, curricular activities and programs designed to raise students' self-esteem and promote team teaching, collaborative learning, and interdisciplinary studies began making inroads into the classroom.

The term "open education" has at least two distinct meanings in the history of 20th-century education. The phrase has been applied both to the inquiry-based child-centered movement that reemerged in the early 1970s and to a particular architectural philosophy and style in the history of school and classroom design. Whereas the child-centered movement emphasizes methodological reforms—it proposes that children should direct their own learning within the context of a decentralized learning environment (see Figure 4.6)—the architectural manifestation of open

FIGURE 4.6. Large tables for activity-based group work take the place of rows of individual student desks in this child-centered classroom. Activity supplies and bins for student work are stored in shelving along the walls.

education attempted explicitly to transform the physical environments of classrooms in the name of better teaching and learning conditions.

Open Plan Learning

Opening plan learning is rooted in the belief that students should be active participants in planning their education. This approach arises in contradiction to the direct instruction approach, which argues that teachers should bear primary or even sole responsibility for organizing the learning experiences of students. Both movements claim a fundamental respect for students, but supporters of open plan learning interpret this respect to include the right of students to make genuine but responsible choices related to how they learn. In her survey of the open plan philosophy, Barbara Blitz (1973, p. 3) outlines a number of the open movement's basic principles:

- children have the right to pursue their individual interests and activities
- in order for meaningful learning to occur, children need to be actively engaged with their environment and other people
- children learn at their own pace and through their own particular learning styles
- learning should be exciting and enjoyable
- the teacher's role should be that of diagnostician, guide, and stimulator

Although open plan learning is at its heart a programmatic reform movement, manifestations of this progressive tradition have also influenced the design of learning settings, particularly at the elementary level. An important strand of open-plan learning is the activity center approach in which students, working alone, with partners, or in small groups, move between carefully crafted spaces in a classroom, each of which is assigned a particular activity or subject focus. Individual activity centers are designed in advance by the teacher, sometimes with the participation of students. Typically, activity centers are organized so that each addresses a unique concept, skill, sensory experience, and/or subject area. In an effort to structure the routine of an activity center classroom, students may be responsible for completing one or more tasks at each activity center throughout the school day.

Once a teacher chooses to adopt an activity center approach, making efficient use of the limited space in a classroom emerges as a critical concern (Loughlin & Suina, 1982). There is a need to find places (and containers) to store the dozens of manipulatives and supplies that make up the activity centers themselves. There are choices to be made in how these materials will be used and made available to students. There are choices to be made in organizing the classroom so students can work together (or alone) on tables, in open spaces, or at activity areas. Lois Napier-Anderson (1988), in keeping with the open movement's support for participatory learning, offers the following advice to teachers:

> As soon as you try to set up centers and work areas, you run into the problem of space. . . . Space will be at a premium so every piece of furniture must have a valid purpose. . . . Desks have to be rearranged. . . . Get your pupils to help you make a scale drawing of your room on graph paper mounted on cardboard. Cut out your essential furniture to the same scale and practice arranging the space by using the model. Children will love to help plan the space so that the best arrangement of furniture is assured—without the chaos of actually moving desks first. Make room dividers, or use shelves and other moveable equipment to divide off quiet corners. (pp. 53–55)

The above choices are not to be confused with the open-plan approach to school design, which will be explored below. A centers approach is typically limited to a self-contained classroom, hence the space constraints noted above. Open-plan schools, on the other hand, are the net result of a facilitywide revamping of the traditional egg-carton layout of classrooms into separate rooms. While both approaches have implications for learning and teaching, only the open-plan school design directly impacts on the way in which students and teachers in multiple classes work and learn together.

Open-Plan Schools

In an effort to counter the stifling limits imposed by the traditional arrangement of classrooms into discrete and isolated cells, some proponents of open-plan learning in the 1960s sought to complement their methodological plans for schools with architectural reforms that promoted team teaching, interdisciplinary learning, student collaboration, and multigrade grouping. In taking their cue from post–World War II British experiences in progressive education, coupled with the support of architects who saw an efficiency and cost benefit to open-plan designs, many progressive educators began espousing the promise of "schooling without walls." Child education was to occur in large open areas in which multiple classes could simultaneously be conducted (see Figure 4.7). Flexible learning spaces, complete with movable dividers, interchangeable storage components, and easily relocatable furniture, were to be the hallmark of modern education. An open and adaptable learning environment was judged to be key in providing an optimum setting for learning. Throughout the late 1960s and early 1970s, school administrators and architects took these pronouncements to heart. Close to 50% of new schools built during this period adopted an open-plan design (Lackney, 1994).

A typical open-plan school would place teachers and students in a large, often circular-shaped room. Using portable dividers and shelving units, the carpeted room would be partitioned pie-style into individual learning spaces with each "slice" belonging to a particular teacher, subject, and/or grade level. A common resource area where each learning space came together in the middle of the room would house library and audio-visual resources for students and administrative space for teachers. Classes would be conducted simultaneously in each section of the room (commonly referred to as a "pod") and the open and flexible layout of the space would encourage student collaboration, team teaching, and interdisciplinary learning.

FIGURE 4.7. Elementary school students are taught in a large partitioned open space. Despite the unique learning setting, it is a direct instruction approach to learning in which students are engaged.

In reviewing the merits of the open-plan design, Basil Castaldi (1987) points to the following advantages:

> The large expanse of space is psychologically liberating. One feels free in both movement and thought. Since partitions are often light, movable visual screens, the spaces for instruction can be changed in size and shape—at will and at once. The omission of walls allegedly reduces the cost of the building substantially. The open space plan lends a feeling of informality to the learning process. Students feel less regimented. There is likely to be a greater intermingling of both students and teachers. The open-space plan facilitates the grouping and regrouping of students and tends to encourage change, experimentation, and innovation. (p. 133)

Although there is general agreement that open-plan schools, when effectively implemented, promote peer interaction and cooperation between teachers (Gump & Ross, 1979), research on other aspects of the open-plan tradition in education has resulted in (at best) mixed results. For example, a Canadian survey of over 100 teachers working in open-plan schools listed the sharing of ideas and materials, team teaching, multigrade grouping, and enhanced support from colleagues to be among the strengths of the open-plan setting. However, this study also highlighted teachers' concerns related to high levels of noise and distraction, occasional disagreements with colleagues, and reduced spontaneity in teaching (Stennett & Earl, 1983). Similarly, while open-plan schools were lauded for promoting team teaching and collaborative learning, the high levels of noise and distraction in these schools prevented such goals from being fully realized (Gump & Ross, 1979)

The open-plan movement is dismissed by most parents, teachers, and educational policy makers today. At best, it is judged to be a well-meaning but poorly implemented reform agenda in an otherwise laudable history of educational innovation. At worst, it is viewed as a hopelessly misguided agenda that at one time jeopardized our children's educational future. In part, the contempt with which the open-plan tradition is now held can be attributed to the revival of a more conservative agenda for schools, an agenda that arguably views the classroom as a unit of economic productivity, rather than a community of learners. Yet this ideological rationalization does not begin to explain the numerous research studies that equate open-space classrooms with reduced task involvement, poor academic performance, and eroded teacher support.

The basic criticism that has been made of open-space classrooms is that they were just too noisy and filled with distraction for students to be able to learn effectively (Bennett et al., 1980). Children with attention deficit disorder and other learning disabilities in particular found it difficult to concentrate for even moderate periods of time. When a lesson demanded concentration or was judged by students to be boring, the more interesting lesson being taught on the other side of the room would often attract their attention (Castaldi, 1987). Also, many open-plan schools lacked semienclosed areas, set away from the high activity levels of highly trafficked spaces, where children could go for privacy, to read a book, or work silently without distraction (see Figure 4.8). In part, the lack of private spaces was congruent with the basic tenets of the open philosophy, which equated successful learning with observable activity and thus deemphasized opportunities for privacy, contemplation, and aloneness time (Hutchison, 1998). As Henry Sanoff (1994) writes:

> Opportunities for privacy, which are never substantial in traditional school buildings, were less available in open areas. Privacy has been shown to con-

FIGURE 4.8. Many teachers attempted to mitigate the primary challenge of open-plan schools—disruptive noise from other classes—by erecting partitions wherever they could.

tribute to a child's growth and development . . . and consequently opportunities for increased privacy, such as secluded areas, have been recommended especially for reading. . . . [Although they] might prefer spaces that are not visibly isolated or cut off from view, students appreciate an environment that provides a variety of places to allow different learning experiences to occur.

Despite the severity of the above problems, the open-plan design may have been doomed to fail for an even more fundamental reason. In an effort to refrain from codifying open education, many supporters of open reforms endeavored to preserve the ambiguity of the term "open" as a way of building solidarity between a diversity of educational agendas. Rather than simply state what open education was, some supporters instead chose to define open education in a negative way, in terms of what it was not (Spodek, 1975). As a result, the relationship between the programmatic reforms of open-plan learning and the architectural reforms of open-plan schools was never fully articulated. Opportunities to reorganize the traditional routines of open-plan schools and harness the group dynamics of open classes were missed. Teacher in-servicing needs went unmet. Administrative leadership was lacking. Without a clear methodological vision and adequate programmatic support, many teachers fell back on traditional instructional techniques. Yet these same teachers continued to believe that they were practicing open education since they were teaching in an open environment.

Open plan schools were also at times presented by designers and administrators as a fait accompli. The physical rearrangement of space in many of these schools represented the end—rather than the beginning—of the reform process. As Jeffery A. Lackney (1994) notes:

> The problem of what constituted open education and open classrooms became a stumbling block very early in the educational reform process for proponents, educational administrators, researchers and designers alike. No clear relationship has ever been presented between open education and the need for open classrooms. . . . Once the open education philosophy took hold, so in turn did the construction of open classrooms. It could be argued that at times the reverse scenario occurred. Open classrooms were constructed with the thought that open education would [naturally] follow. This scenario constituted a naive environmental determinism: that the physical environment can determine behavior. (p. 53)

Although the impulse to purposefully design schools that put 1,000 students in the equivalent of one room is no longer with us, the legacy of open-plan schools still has an impact on education today. Many schools that saw a return to a more traditional one-classroom-for-30-students design in the 1980s were required to implement such reforms in schools that were originally constructed to support open-plan learning. Today, with the important exception of a few public (alternative) schools, the legacy of open-plan reforms in many school districts is a mixed bag of traditional and innovative school design coupled with renovations, additions, and space reallocation initiatives aimed at returning schools to their traditional egg-carton layout.

THE NATURAL ENVIRONMENT

Although the proponents of open-plan schools radically overhauled the interior of schools, they never left the building to explore the learning potential of the open environment outside of the school. It would not be until the early 1980s that just such a task would be undertaken by environmental educators, as well as small groups of parents and teachers intent on building stronger school/community ties in their local neighborhoods. School ground naturalization, a grassroots ecological restoration movement for schools, emerged from these early efforts to become, by the end of the 20th century, arguably the fastest growing environmental education initiative throughout the world.

School ground naturalization programs restore all or part of the playground and other areas surrounding a school to their natural state through the reintroduction of plant species that are indigenous to the local area. In the last 2 decades, hundreds of elementary, secondary, and postsecondary schools in the United States and around the world have initiated naturalization projects that aim to enhance aesthetically a school's outside environment and provide quality outdoor learning experiences for students (Evergreen Foundation, 1994). Significantly, these projects have tended to be grassroots initiatives rather than top-down mandated reforms. Working together, teachers, students, parents, local businesspeople, and community residents have designed vegetable and herb gardens, bird and butterfly habitats, prairie gardens, and woodland forests; and built outdoor classrooms (see Figure 4.9), amphitheaters, tree houses, and other play and learning environments to complement these naturalized spaces.

Although school-based ecological restoration efforts have undergone a resurgence since the early 1980s, efforts to transform school grounds into naturalized spaces for children and adults are not entirely new. Since the mid-18th century, naturalization initiatives in American schools have variously aimed to beautify school grounds, promote child health through play in nature, and provide integrated outdoor learning experiences that complement the education that students receive indoors. At the dawn of the 20th century, school gardens were favored for their ability to shield students and teachers from the heat of summer (and the cold of winter), and they played a key role in teaching civic virtues through children's gardening endeavors (Coffey, 1996). However, by the mid-20th century, naturalized spaces were being replaced with concrete play areas and the formal planting of trees and grasses (which perhaps reflected a postwar longing for order and control). Only in recent years have school ground naturalization initiatives again garnered attention. A revived interest in environmental education, coupled with a mounting concern for declining natural spaces in cities, has prompted a renewed interest in the school grounds as a naturalized outdoor area for play, learning, and reflection. The success of ecological restoration efforts—by the late 1990s over one third of schools in Britain alone hosted naturalized spaces—has helped the school ground naturalization movement to quickly become one of the most influential environmental education strategies around the world.

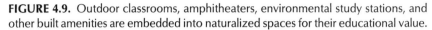

FIGURE 4.9. Outdoor classrooms, amphitheaters, environmental study stations, and other built amenities are embedded into naturalized spaces for their educational value.

Supporters of ecological restoration initiatives argue that such projects bring nature back into the city; provide students, teachers, and local residents with opportunities for daily contact with nature; serve as living examples of developing ecosystems; provide naturalized play and learning spaces for children; and serve as immediately accessible field study centers for hands-on environmental education activities (Evergreen Foundation, 1994). Above all, such projects help foster a healthy appreciation of nature and enhance a sense of community in the surrounding neighborhood.

There are also economic factors at work. In many school districts, environmental education today faces serious setbacks as natural spaces within urban communities disappear and as school budgets are cut back significantly. Although most school districts pay lip service to environmental education goals, the traditional practice of sending students on periodic day or overnight visits to outdoor education centers is now judged by many to be no longer financially feasible. Other options for environmental education need to be considered, especially a strengthening of environmental education programs within urban communities. School ground naturalization projects aim to complement periodic day and overnight trips to outdoor education centers, by bringing nature back into the city and functioning as year-round centers for ongoing environmental education in schools. Perhaps most importantly, these projects reinforce the idea that nature and humans can coexist in cities and grow and flourish together.

It goes without saying that ecological restoration projects can have dramatic implications for the experience of place in (and around) schools. It is with an enhanced sense of pride that schools (often in the spring) show off a newly naturalized area of their site. Yet a naturalization project is never truly complete—school gardens require continuous care and maintenance—so it is the long-term involvement of teachers, students, parents, and local residents in the process of restoring and sustaining a site that often builds a sense of community. A serious challenge for many schools is to maintain the momentum once a project is underway (Hutchison, 1999). In part, this can be achieved by fostering strong curricular connections between a naturalized site and the rest of the going-ons in the school (Reading & Taven, 1996).

To help foster solid curricular connections, many naturalized spaces are purposely crafted to include a number of play and learning amenities that encourage the regular use of the site by students and teachers. Naturalized spaces may be variously designed to promote differentiated, flexible, and year-round use, as well as age-appropriate challenge for students (Moore & Wong, 1997). Some naturalized sites feature shelter or shade, a sitting area for a full class (or a lone student), and/or signage and pathways that direct visitors. Schools throughout North America have selectively turned naturalized spaces into multiuse places by building outdoor classrooms, environmental science stations, tree houses, and amphitheaters (see Figure 4.10). Similarly, pathways and log benches for conducting site tours, lessons, and group discussions are integrated into the design of many sites. To underscore the ecological principles at work, some naturalized schools have implemented composting programs to put food scraps and other waste to good use.

In addition to articulating the curricular goals for the project, selecting an appropriate location for a naturalized space is a critical first step in any naturalization program. Experienced naturalization proponents advise schools to start small, to focus the first year on a small corner of a chosen site, and then grow the naturalized space over successive seasons. Perhaps most importantly, schools are advised to choose low-traffic sites that are unfrequented by students and staff. Naturalized sites that are located in highly trafficked areas, such as the immediate vicinity of a main

FIGURE 4.10. If vandalism and theft is a concern, a school's courtyard can instead be transformed into a naturalized space.

roadway, sports field, or parking lot may be more visible to students and the general public, but such spaces won't necessarily fare well in the long run. They may even invite vandalism, which is an ongoing concern for all naturalized sites, regardless of location.

Despite this advice, some schools have purposefully located their naturalized spaces in the highly trafficked areas of school grounds, in effect transforming the daily place experience of students and staff. Rather than locate all of their naturalized sites in out-of-the-way locations, far removed from the play life of children, the project leaders at BroadAcres Elementary School in Toronto, for example, chose to integrate the playground and naturalized spaces of their school:

> In addition to a naturalized space which is located in the school's courtyard
> . . . BroadAcres School has also purposefully integrated naturalized spaces
> into the middle of the children's playground area. In this area, each class
> has cultivated its own garden plot and [newly planted] trees are protected

by natural barriers—minigardens that surround the trees and protect their root systems from being trampled on. . . . Log benches with built-in checkerboards also add to the utility of this space. In contrast, the Old Orchard and W. A. Porter schools chose a site which was set off from those areas that attract a lot of traffic. . . . The Old Orchard community naturalized the perimeter of their school by turning the original concrete hill surrounding the playground into a terrace garden. The W. A. Porter community naturalized a corner area of their school that was enclosed on three sides, protected from the elements, and used infrequently by students. An out-of-the-way area where teachers and students could purposefully go to "do naturalization" was found to be more preferable for these two schools. (Hutchison, 1999, pp. 4–5)

Despite the school ground naturalization movement's success, few studies have explored the impact of naturalized play spaces on children's place perceptions (e.g., Bell, 2001; Center for Ecoliteracy, 1999; Harvey, 1989; Moore, 1989; Moore & Wong, 1997). Most literature tends to be anecdotal, qualitative, or instructional in nature. Of particular note is Wendy Titman's (1994) research on elementary schools in Britain. Titman found that naturalized sites were heavily favored by children over the concrete playgrounds that they replaced. The various nooks and crannies of naturalized sites invited children's exploration. Grass was symbolic of "gentle game space . . . trees of climbing . . . and flowers of aesthetic values" (pp. 35–39). Children reported that tending a garden enhanced their sense of pride and deepened their connection to the school as a whole. Titman concludes that all school grounds, whether naturalized or not, are "read" by children as they would read any external environment—as places to value, respond to, and utilize in certain ways. As with the other educational movements explored in this chapter, ecological restoration efforts recognize the importance of consciously designed learning spaces for children. Such spaces evoke a certain set of responses in both students and teachers and aim for congruence with the educational philosophies with which they are allied.

THE PHILOSOPHY OF CLASSROOM DESIGN

The Montessori, Waldorf, open-plan, and school ground naturalization movements each argue for a unique and innovative design plan for schools, classrooms, and/or outdoor spaces. Yet at their core, each shares a similar concern for the need to consciously plan learning settings for children. The first principles of all four reform traditions might fairly be described as follows:

- young children require a planned learning environment and routine
- this learning environment should be separate from the work and learning environments of adults
- adults can construct such an environment to support children's learning

The above principles reinforce the view that consciously planned learning environments for children are important. Moreover, the planning of children's learning settings requires special considerations related to children's developmental experience and the unique curricular goals of child education.

That child education should occur separately from the education of adults is itself an ideological statement that flies in the face of deschooling proposals such as the one presented in the next chapter. As Montessori notes:

> The first essential for the child's development is concentration. It lays the whole basis for his character and social behavior. . . . [Hence] the importance of his surroundings . . . [where] the importance of our schools really lies. They are places in which the child can find the kind of work that permits him to do this . . . Our schools offer the tinies a sheltering refuge in which the first elements of character can take shape. (1995, p. 222)

Each of the above philosophies argues that adults are in a position to make decisions on behalf of children as to just what an ideal childhood learning environment comprises. Even open-plan schools, which historically valued children's freedom, did not give children a choice as to whether or not they would be educated in an open-plan setting. For these schools, the open-plan setting was a given. What children and teachers collaboratively did to further define the open-plan environment occurred within this given physical and ideological context.

The above similarities notwithstanding, there are also a number of conceptual dichotomies that further frame some of the differences between the four educational movements. By stepping back to view each movement from a distance—from a metaperspective, as it were—it is possible to further articulate the relationship between educational ideology and the construction of place in schools. This chapter closes by addressing three such conceptual dichotomies: positive versus negative freedom, the explicit versus implicit curriculum, and the organic versus synthetic aesthetic.

Positive versus Negative Freedom

Throughout most of the 20th century, the place of freedom in education constituted one of the most controversial ideas in educational philosophy. The issue of just how much freedom students should enjoy in schools has been tackled by leading educational thinkers as diverse as John Dewey (1938/1963), A. S. Neill (1960), and Paulo Freire (1984), among others. So, too, the idea of freedom is central to the four philosophies reviewed in this chapter, particularly those advanced by Maria Montessori, Rudolf Steiner, and the proponents of open-plan learning. It is perhaps ironic, given the concerns of her movement's critics, that it is Maria Montessori who has arguably put forward the most scathing critique of teacher authority in traditional education. In what might fairly be described as an over-the-top caricature of turn-of-the-19th-century education, Montessori wrote:

> In all pedagogy up to our own time, the word education has been almost synonymous with the word punishment. . . . Those delicate, trembling limbs are held to the wood for more than three hours of anguish, three and three of many days and months and years. The child's hands are fastened to the desk by stern . . . looks . . . and when into the mind a thirst for truth and knowledge the ideas of the teacher are forcibly driven . . . the little head [lies] humbled in submission. (Montessori, 1936/1963, pp. 281–282)

Yet just how immune is the Montessori method from somewhat more reserved criticisms when it comes to freedom in education? It seems clear that teacher authority is not the issue, for teachers working within the Montessori tradition make every effort to stay out of the way of children who are busy at work with the various manipulatives that comprise the instructional program; and yet, as was noted earlier in this chapter, there is an overt environmental authority at work in Montessori preschools in the form of the prepared environment which structures and limits child behavior and fraternization. As Valerie Polakow (1992) notes:

> Montessori believed that satisfying engagement and absorption in work led to the formulation of a system of inner controls, a sense of personal fulfill-ment which facilitated the development of an inner strength and self-discipline. (p. 82)

This is the essence of positive freedom—the notion that hard work, restraint, and/or sacrifice will over time nurture an autonomous learner who is free from the whim, caprice, and impulse-driven behavior of the undisciplined child (Lankshear, 1982). This view of freedom is shared by traditional, Montessori, and, in many respects, Waldorf education and it is in sharp contrast to the negative notion of freedom, which underlies the relaxed authority of the open-plan philosophy (and free schools such as Summerhill). In moving away from traditional education, Montessori and Steiner framed the need for authority in childhood education in terms of a developmental imperative rather than an ideological dictum. Montessori, in particular, articulated a deeply felt philosophy that equated freedom with a structured environment and disciplined interaction with specially constructed learning materials. Discipline, intellectual focus, individual work, and mind are all intricately interwoven in Montessori's early childhood philosophy, the effective implementation of which leads to a sense of self-fulfillment and a free-thinking adult:

> The [Montessori] environment and materials have controls built into them to eliminate obstacles, to encourage beneficial activities, and to correct the child's errors. The spontaneous use of these auto-instructional materials enables the child to focus his attention upon the mastery of subjects and skills. Each child should be given the opportunity to work *freely* in self-chosen tasks commensurate with his needs. (Hainstock, 1986, p. 68, italics added)

The use of the word "freely" in the above passage betrays the notion of freedom forwarded by open education and other, more radical, free schooling traditions, but it reinforces the positive notion of freedom and authority that is supported, perhaps to varying degrees, by both Montessori and Waldorf education. For Montessori educators, freedom is rooted in the structuredness of the prepared environment. For Waldorf educators, freedom is rooted in the strength of the child-teacher relationship.

Explicit versus Implicit Curriculum

In most educational philosophies, there is both an implicit and explicit curriculum at work with regard to educating students. Critical educators typically point to inequities in the choices and roles that are subconsciously assigned to students on the basis of class, race, and gender, but there are also other "hidden" forces at work, including an implicit curriculum that in part comprises the subconscious influence of environmental design on child behavior and development:

> Those who design spaces in which children will spend many hours a day, at an age in which the brain, the body, and the feelings are so extraordinarily reactive and undergoing rapid formation, must be aware of the possibilities that the space offers children for expressing and developing all their genetic

equipment, as well as the restrictions created by the space and that which it denies. The spaces, materials, colors, light, microclimate, and furnishings must be direct and integral participants in the great alchemy of growing within a community. (Vecchi, 1998, p. 135)

The notion of an implicit or hidden environmental curriculum is most pronounced in Waldorf education where the learning environment is consciously designed by educators to deepen the interior lives of both students and teachers. The influence of the school environment on the interior life of the child is judged to be subconscious and spiritual. Unlike the Montessori notion of the prepared environment, it is not explicitly taught to children or otherwise made overt; rather, the aesthetic character of the Waldorf school complements the arts-based instruction that comprises the explicit curriculum. In this way, the aesthetics of Waldorf pedagogy and place complement one another by working toward a common goal on conscious and subconscious levels, respectively.

For school ground naturalization proponents, on the other hand, the learning environment *is* the curriculum, and this explicit curriculum is clear to all. Creating an outdoor learning environment—that is, growing and nurturing the school gardens—constitutes environmental education which, in turn, infers a design partnership between teachers, students, and other adults. It can be said that the curriculum of a naturalized school literally grows out of the design of the learning environment. Choices are made to create this or that habitat, pathway, outdoor classroom, or other learning amenity and the garden itself serves as the impetus for further learning.

Organic versus Synthetic Aesthetics

Ever since Friedrich Froebel invented the kindergarten over a century and a half ago, there has been a strong affinity for beauty in childhood learning environments. This tradition continues today in both Waldorf education and the school ground naturalization movement, which perhaps comes closer than any other educational philosophy to literally embracing Froebel's 19th-century vision of a "garden of children." Froebel argued for a childhood aesthetic which reflected the romantic ideals of innocence and nature; hence the strong organic character of both Waldorf education and the school ground naturalization movement. For Froebel, the marriage of childhood and nature served, in part, as an educational defense against the corrupting influence of society. (This was a carryover of Rousseau's thought.) Waldorf education, in turn, strengthens the child-nature relationship by situating it within the context of a holistic developmental theory. In Waldorf education, the aesthetics of childhood, the learning environment, and curriculum aim to be one and the same, with each complementing the others.

Although beauty in non-Waldorf childhood settings is common, organic beauty is not. In our modern-day petroleum-based culture, it is plastic that has come to define the material makeup and aesthetics of most child care centers and elementary school classrooms. Long gone are wooden toys and hand-woven dolls. The sandbox and water table take a backseat to intricately designed toys and manipulatives, such as battery-operated cars and play sets that mimic (to the last detail) their real-world counterparts. The organic aesthetics of natural hues and washed-out watercolors are replaced by brightly colored walls, toys, and spot-color posters. Favored in most schools is an organizational aesthetic that arguably values presentation and efficiency over participation and imagination.

Chapter 5

NO PLACE LIKE CYBERSPACE

I believe that the motion picture is destined to revolutionize our educational system and that in a few years, it will supplant largely, if not entirely, the use of textbooks. . . . The education of the future, as I see it, will be conducted through the medium of the motion picture.
—Thomas Edison (1922)

A technological revolution is sweeping through the U. S. and world econo-mies that is totally transforming the social role of learning and teaching. This learning revolution already has made the "classroom teacher" as obsolete as the blacksmith shop. . . . The nations that stop trying to "reform" their education and training institutions and choose instead to totally replace them with a brand-new, high-tech learning system will be the world's economic powerhouses through the twenty-first century.
—Lewis J. Perelman (1992, p. 20)

Chapter 4 traced the ideological lines of thought that run through four educational movements. At the heart of each movement is a particular construction of place that is intricately related to a specific vision of child-hood, learning, and curriculum. Yet despite their divergent educational proposals, each movement takes as its starting point a common understand-ing of place. Learning, in the eyes of the Montessori, Waldorf, open-plan school, and naturalization traditions, occurs in the real world and is the result of face-to-face interactions between children, teachers, and curricular materials situated in physical learning settings.

Until the mid-20th century, only our imaginations would allow us to conceive of an interactive educational setting that was not based in the physical world. Yet with the advent of computers, and subsequent advances in simulation, virtual reality, and digital telecommunication technologies, the ability to educate children in virtual learning settings is being seriously studied and heralded by some as the harbinger of a new educational re-naissance with clear implications for both pedagogy and place.

111

THE HISTORICAL ROOTS OF INSTRUCTIONAL TECHNOLOGY

The computer was not the first electronic technology to make its mark on education (see Figure 5.1). Early in the 20th century, proponents of instructional technology promoted the use of film and radio in classrooms, and (as the opening quotation of this chapter indicates) some reformers foresaw a technological revolution in education stemming from such advancements.

Advocates of instructional technology saw an efficiency benefit to the use of film and radio. As an outgrowth of progressivism and the scientific management of schools (Cuban, 1986), the application of technology to classrooms held the promise of boosting teaching productivity and lowering the long-term costs of delivering educational programs (short-term startup costs for equipment purchases notwithstanding). Just as the classroom computer would later become a symbol of cutting-edge innovation

FIGURE 5.1. Stored away in many schools is evidence of an instructional technology age long gone. Yet how long will it be before the desktop computer (top right) joins the record player and film strip projector?

in the 1980s and beyond, so the film projector served as a symbol of classroom modernity throughout the 1920s and 1930s. As with recent research into the use of computers in schools, early research on the effectiveness of film concluded that instruction via film was either superior to or as effective as the traditional instructional approaches it augmented or replaced (Wise, 1939).

Despite the positive research results, film never received the widespread adoption that its advocates had hoped for. Many teachers lacked the necessary skills to operate film projectors. There was also the high cost of building both a film library and purchasing and maintaining film projectors and screens to consider. Finally, the high cost of equipment resulted in an unmanageable teacher-to-film projector ratio. Film projectors were not conveniently available when teachers needed them. These concerns, insofar as they relate to technical competence, cost, and accessibility, have changed little even as the focus of educational technology has shifted to the personal computer in recent decades.

During this early period, radio seemed to fare somewhat better. By the late 1930s, early technical problems with radio sets had been fixed and over 50% of American schools owned at least one set (Woelfel & Tyler, 1945). Soon, both local and national radio stations began to produce educational radio content for schools. However, despite this effort, the early promise of a radio in every classroom was not to be. Only 7% of respondents in a nationwide 1937 survey reported that all classrooms in their school used radio (Atkinson, 1938), and the percentage was still less in rural areas. In reviewing the early adoption of radio in schools, Woelfel and Tyler (1945, p. 73) attribute the failure of radio education to teachers' "indifference and lethargy, even antagonism toward this revolutionary means of communication," as well as the "fixed courses of study and rules of conduct" in schools, a critique that would again be given voice years later by some cyberschooling reformers (e.g., Perelman, 1992).

Unwilling to give up on new forms of instructional technology, supporters of radio in schools eagerly waited for the widespread adoption of educational television, an inevitability in one supporter's view that was sure to bridge the "blindness gap" that marred the early adoption of radio (Darrow, 1932, p. 266). Unlike film and radio, television received substantial support from the private sector, most notably from the Ford Foundation, which throughout the 1950s invested over $20 million dollars to support educational television initiatives in some 250 U. S. school districts (Ford Foundation, 1961). Financial support from the federal government soon followed, so that by the early 1970s over $100 million had been invested in educational television by the private and public sectors (Cuban, 1986). Such early partnerships between school districts and private enterprise would come to serve as noteworthy models for more recent school-business partnerships, which aim to equip schools with the latest in computer technology.

THE RISE OF THE NET GENERATION

At their core, film, radio, and television share a critical limitation. They are noninteractive technologies. The transmission of information moves one way—from source to student. Just as overcoming radio's "blindness gap" was judged to be key to the success of educational television in the early 20th century, so did the need to move instructional technology into a new interactive learning realm in the 1980s (the nondigital teaching machines of the 1960s and 1970s notwithstanding) signal, for early cyberschooling proponents, a revolution in education from which we have yet to emerge.

Over the last 2 decades, there have been two computer revolutions of major significance to education. The first occurred in the late 1970s and early 1980s, spurred by the introduction of the personal computer. Marketed first to businesses and, shortly thereafter, to homes and schools, the IBM PC and Apple II computers heralded the promise of an individually scaled technology that could deliver one-to-one educational instruction to students. Throughout the 1980s, school computers were used for administrative purposes, to provide drill and remedial instruction to students, and to teach basic programming skills using tools such as BASIC, HyperCard, and LOGO. Proponents touted the efficiency of computers and pointed to the technologization of the workplace as important rationales for introducing computers into the curriculum. Computers were deemed to be infinitely "patient," and therefore ideally suited to matching the varied learning paces of students.

The earliest personal computers served three basic functions: information storage, processing, and retrieval. Yet with the exception of a minority of networked labs, computers were isolated from each other and missing a key educational ingredient: namely, communication. For educators, the early promise of computers that could communicate with one another was heralded by a 1983 magazine advertisement from Apple. Featuring a contrasting mix of the traditional and innovative, the ad depicted a top-down view of a networked classroom, traditionally arranged into rows of students facing a teacher, but with a computer on every child's desk.

Despite the early forays into networked educational computing, the notion of the computer as a learning tool for communicating with the outside world did not take off until the popularization of the Internet in 1994. By simply adding an inexpensive modem to a computer system, even novice computer users could set up networked access to the outside world using a basic phone line. From there, access to Web sites, e-mail, and chat rooms was only an Internet provider and software download away. The Internet was originally designed in 1969 to serve as a communications backbone for the U. S. defense industry and later, in the 1980s, university science and technology departments (Winston, 1998); but in 1993, with the release of Mosaic, the first user-friendly and widely available Internet browser, the World Wide Web took off as if satisfying some pent-up public and private enterprise need for a new worldwide telecommunications medium.

Today, much of the media hype surrounding the integration of computers into schools has less to do with computers per se and more to do with the Internet as a vast worldwide resource for students. Hence, for educational technology advocates, the call for schoolwide access to the Internet represents the second educational computer revolution in as many decades. In the eyes of many cyberschooling proponents, the computer has been transformed from a one-to-one teaching machine into a specialized communications switchboard that allows students to browse for and publish information and communicate with peers and adults around the world.

VISIONS OF A CYBERSCHOOLING FUTURE

Foremost among a variety of proposals for integrating computers into education are two plans that call for a major overhaul of the educational process as we now know it. The first plan extends from the current effort to wire every U. S. school and put a computer on every child's desk. The second and more radical plan embraces the vision of a deschooled society in which K–12 schools are deemed unnecessary and purposeless.

Wiring the Nation's Schools

The current effort to wire every U. S. school was framed in Chapter 3 as a school design initiative aimed at modernizing the infrastructure of school buildings. Yet, at its core, this initiative is a philosophical rather than an architectural reform. As such, it has significant implications for curriculum, teaching, and learning. In order to prepare children for life in the 21st century and future high-tech employment, cyberschooling proponents argue that it is necessary to transform the tools of teaching from textbooks and chalkboards to computers and the World Wide Web. Typically, the rationale for schoolwide Internet access goes something like this:

> Technological literacy is a "new basic" of American education and the Internet is the blackboard of the future. Yet thousands of schools find it difficult to provide the powerful learning opportunities afforded by technology because they lack the basic electrical wiring and phone lines necessary to plug in computers and connect them to the Internet. As we repair and replace dilapidated and unsafe schools, we must ensure that they are "21st century schools." This means wires, electrical capacity, electrical outlets, and cable and telephone lines that will allow students to take full advantage of the learning opportunities that technology offers. (U. S. Department of Education, 1997, p. 1)

Or sometimes like this:

> Technological literacy—meaning computer skills and the ability to use computers and other technology to improve learning, productivity, and performance—has become as fundamental to a person's ability to navigate through society as traditional skills like reading, writing, and arithmetic. Yet, for the most part, these new technologies are not to be found in the nation's schools. Students make minimal use of new technologies for learning, typically employing them for only a few minutes a day. Indeed, the hard realities are that only 4 percent of schools have a computer for every five students (a ratio deemed adequate to allow regular use) and only 9 percent of classrooms are connected to the Internet. In schools with large concentrations of low-income students, the numbers are often even lower. Research and the experiences of schools in the forefront of the current "digital revolution," however, underscore the enormous learning opportunities available through technology. (U. S. Department of Education, 1996, p. 1)

As the above quotations indicate, the U. S. government is on board as a supporter of the high-tech wiring of schools. Indeed, the goal of Internet access for every classroom was among the Clinton administration's top policy priorities for education.

The federal initiative to wire U. S. schools has four components. First, there is the basic effort, now underway in a majority of states, to connect every school to the Internet. Second, there is the goal of bridging the technology gap between rich and poor by ensuring that every child has access to modern computer technology. Third, there is the ongoing goal of providing teachers with technology-related training and inservicing. (Here there is a need to help teachers get up to speed on new instructional technologies. Instructional proficiency requires a degree of technical competence, but also a solid grounding in how to successfully integrate technology into the curriculum.) Finally, there is the goal of supporting the development of high-quality digital content in the form of instructional tools, multimedia titles, age- and grade-appropriate software, and "kid-safe" educational Web sites.

Deschooling Society

In the debate over the future of technology in education, the plan to wire every U. S. school represents the moderate reform position. Teachers, in the view of the above plan's proponents, retain a critical role in child education as, to a lesser extent, do textbooks and other curricular materials that are rooted in the "real world." Children continue to go to school, so the physical infrastructure of schools as formal institutions dedicated to the education of the young stays in place.

The contrary position argues that the technological revolution on which our society is currently embarking necessitates a full-scale revamping of the way that children learn, including where and how they learn. In the very near future, so the argument goes, there will be no need for schools as we now know them. Each day, children and adults will log online to the information superhighway (likely from home) and participate, essentially as equals, in on-line discussion forums, virtual reality explorations, and other computer-mediated instructional pursuits.

This future technological vision of a deschooled society is perhaps forwarded most forcefully by Lewis J. Perelman, whose 1992 book argues that schools are not and never again will be conducive to the technological revolution we are now experiencing. Perelman outlines his argument for a transformation in the conditions of learning and teaching as follows:

- Although learning and teaching used to be a solely human process, learning has recently become a transhuman process that partners humans with powerful neural networks, expert systems, and automated learning machines.
- Society used to be able to define education as something that occurred solely in the classroom, cut off from the rest of the world. Today, however, education permeates almost every aspect of a person's social, work, leisure, and home life. In the private sector, education is already a big business—witness the rise of private professional and technical schools, educational television networks, and teaching software. Succeeding within the world of work means

committing to lifelong learning, including on-the-job training and
the personal upgrading of employment skills.
* Learning can no longer be construed as the one-way dissemina-
tion of knowledge from teacher and textbook to student. In the
information age, everyone is a learner and there are no teaching
experts per se. So, too, the shelf life of up-to-date knowledge has
shrunk, in many instances, from several years to only weeks or
days. A new global telecommunications system that can manage,
update, and instantly deliver information to students is required.

Educators might wish to counter each of the above points—Perelman
does seem to subscribe to an antiquated notion of just what occurs in
schools and he doesn't adequately address the unique psychosocial needs
of children or the socioemotional aims of child education, which cannot
be so easily transferred into explicit computerized data—but the allure
of his proposals do attract a following among many business leaders, technological innovators, and critics of the educational establishment.

So just what do Perelman and other like-minded deschooling proponents propose? First, Perelmen argues that public education must be
privatized and deinstitutionalized. Perelman is a staunch capitalist and
he sees public education as the last of the world's major socialist institutions. Furthermore, he argues that if we retain the status quo, educational bureaucrats, teacher's unions, school districts, and teacher training
institutions, will only slow down the pace of reform and stand in the way
of technological and social progress. Instead, we need to transfer public
monies that are normally spent on K–12 education into new technology
innovation funds that will help build the new on-line and privatized telecommunications infrastructure that will support learning in the 21st
century.

Second, Perelman argues that we need to outlaw credentialism (i.e.,
the right of employers to discriminate against applicants on the basis of
the number and level of degrees they have). Credentialism, Perelman
argues, is the primary means by which schools, particularly colleges and
universities, extend their monopoly on learning and maintain the financial support of the public. With credentialism outlawed, employers would
rely solely on merit and competence in their hiring practices as measured
by assessment instruments and perhaps a single certificate of basic com-
petency. Young people and even technology-savvy teenagers would be in
a position to compete with older adults for jobs. As Perelman sees it, "[P]ublic
enthusiasm for paying exorbitant taxes and tuition for diploma mills would
wane swiftly" (1992, p. 307).

REENVISIONING PLACE IN THE CYBERSCHOOLING AGE

It is interesting to note that some of what Perelman calls for in his 1992 book, namely a global telecommunications medium and distance learning infrastructure, is now firmly in place in the form of the Internet. Not surprisingly, the Internet has become the de facto focus of a majority of cyberschooling proposals at present, particularly those that aim to capitalize on the agenda of getting American schools on-line. The design and infrastructure challenges of incorporating networked computers into schools was addressed in Chapter 3, but the implications for pedagogy and place go far beyond issues of basic school design. They also include a number of important ideational and pedagogical shifts to our conceptions of place in education and, more generally, everyday life.

The Virtual Construction of Place

The language of place. From its inception, the lexicon of the Internet has co-opted preexisting concepts of place in an effort to make the new familiar and connect emerging technologies to place constructions in the physical world. Internet jargon such as "navigation," "cyberspace," "information superhighway," "Web sites," and "chat rooms" are now used daily by people the world over to describe what they do and where they go as they "travel" the World Wide Web. Navigating from site to site is judged to be the cyber equivalent of traveling from one place to another in the physical world. Recent improvements to the infrastructure of the Internet are now propelling the construction of 3D virtual worlds, such as on-line storefronts, museum walkthroughs, and first-person action game environments. The construction of such spaces further strengthens the cyber place metaphor.

The fluidity of place. Places in the physical world by necessity conform to the physical laws of nature. Columns and beams counter the force of gravity. Enclosed spaces protect us from the elements. Buildings are oriented to let in or keep out sunlight at particular times of the day. Walls mark off the boundaries of rooms. Stairs connect one level of a structure to another. Escalators and elevators provide an efficient means of transport between these levels. Yet in cyberspace, gravity is a nonissue. There is no cold or rain from which to protect ourselves. Virtual sunlight can be pointed anywhere (Mitchell, 1999). Walls can be semipermeable and cyber visitors can be transported instantly from one level of a cyber structure to another. Moreover, virtual spaces can appear and disappear, morph into new spaces, fold into each other, change hues to match our moods, and be programmed to expand or contract to accommodate the height of the virtual visitors who inhabit the space. In short, the design of places in the virtual universe is infinitely variable and free from many of the design restrictions imposed on places in the physical world:

> The spaces made possible by the computer and Internet have no conventional physical dimensions. The Internet . . . consists of many constantly changing spaces. Each space is defined by the communications of its inhabitants . . . The conversation—not traditional physical boundaries, such as walls and ceilings—shapes the "room." When students use the Internet, they become architects of these on-line spaces. (Hird, 2000, pp. 50–51)

The recognition of place. Although they may not heed the physical laws of the universe, designers of cyber places must still be wary of human expectations and comfort levels in relation to place (Qvortrup, 2002). (Alternatively, cyber place designers can attempt, over time, to forge new expectations for virtual places.) Just as in the physical world, visitors to a cyber place expect to find signposts and other visual cues to guide them through an on-line space. Just as most Web pages conform to a design pattern that places a header at the top and button links to the left-hand side, so are well-designed virtual spaces easily recognized and transparently navigated with little effort. And just as in the physical world, cyber places require a clear delineation between public spaces (e.g., where a visitor's movements may be tracked) and private spaces (e.g., where two or more visitors can meet privately and securely).

The Physical Construction of Place

The transparency of place. It is not only the virtual experience of place that may be transformed by emerging high technologies. Advances in computer hardware also hold the promise of transforming our experience of place in the physical world. The design of the personal computer has to date been limited by the need for obtrusive interface tools, such as the keyboard and mouse. The personal computer is almost universally viewed as a self-contained device, explicit and removed from its surroundings, as well defined as a toaster, car, or other single-purpose technology. Yet the computer is a transmutable, multipurpose tool and its form and existence as an explicit component of our surroundings is a cultural construction. With the widespread adoption of voice recognition and speech synthesis technologies, the personal computer may soon fade into the background of our living, working, and learning environments. Wall monitors (and eventually holograms) may, in the not too distant future, provide any

necessary visual output, but the computer itself will speak to us and respond to voice commands as, for example, we walk through the various
rooms in our homes. Personal computers (or their functional equivalents)
will be omnipresent in virtually every place we travel to but, perhaps like
billboards and school bells today, they will exist as taken-for-granted, even
transparent elements of the surrounding environment.

The embodiment of place. Just as the personal computer may soon fade
into the built environment, so too computer chips may soon inhabit our
bodies. No longer just the stuff of science fiction, cyberimplants and
nanoprobes are today the focus of biotech research in emerging technology labs around the world:

> Imagine millions, perhaps billions, of micro- and nanoscopic computing
> machines crawling over your body: in your face, in your eyes and ears, up
> your nose, in your mouth, and down your throat; infesting your lung cavi-
> ties, swimming in your bloodstream and bathing in your fluids. . . . Imag-
> ine, also, the air full of biomechanical objects borne on air and sound
> pressures, some almost invisible, like pollen, others, actually invisible to
> the naked eye, and yet others the size of insects. This will be part of the
> environment of the future, where occluded fronts of biomechanical life forms
> drift or propel themselves within and across bodies and continents. (Spiller,
> 1998, p. 105)

Nanotechnologies not only have the potential to regulate (and repair)
physiological functions, but also to impress themselves upon our consciousness, to transport our senses and cognitive processes instantly from one
place to another. The widespread adoption of the computer chip in the
brain and other embedded technologies may eventually beg the taken-
for-granted answer to the question, Where does my "self" end and the
places I inhabit begin?

The Virtual Construction of Educational Places

The innovation of place. Current and emerging Internet and computer
technologies also hold the promise of directly transforming the experience
of place in education. Video conferencing technologies today allow distance learning courses to be offered to groups of students who are sepa-
rated by wide geographic spaces. Video streams of instruction can be
delivered to students live, in real-time, or on-demand, according to their
needs. From a complementary perspective, simulation technologies
allow students to learn in 3D and through sight, sound, and touch. Students can experience the physical principles of science "firsthand" and take

guided 3D virtual tours of museums and art galleries. Wearing virtual reality technologies such as headsets and gloves, students can explore both micro- and macro-sized worlds, with scales as minute as a microbe or as massive as the universe. Such immersive experiences hold the promise of tapping into all of a student's senses and altering the laws upon which human perception is based in the physical world. Within such a scenario, the experience of place is no longer direct, but mediated by the technology that resides between learner and curriculum.

The reduction of place. There is a caveat to the above. For places (and other cultural knowledge) to be experienced on a virtual level, they must first be transferred to or constructed within the digital realm. This process requires real-world places to be converted into a binary code that treats all knowledge as explicit and which does not capture the full subtlety of human intentionality, emotion, communal memory, and context (Bowers, 2000). All digital representations of information, including movies, audio, and 3D environments are, at their core, 0s and 1s. This is the only language that the computer understands. Digitizing places requires all cultural knowledge about people, places, and societies to be reduced to this binary code. Although concealed by rich multimedia interfaces, the human experience of cyber places is necessarily mediated through the arrangement of place data into the transistor equivalents of "off" and "on."

The scale of place. Coupled with a modem and Internet connection, computers are expanding the notion of where students learn. Before the rise of the Internet, formal education was restricted to the classroom and occasional excursions into the community. Today, however, the world has opened up to students who can travel (metaphorically speaking) to distant lands and learn about faraway cultures by navigating the World Wide Web. Students can access Web content housed in servers around the world, start pen-pal relationships with students in other countries, and participate in chat groups with children and adults scattered around the globe. Internet technology is redefining the relationship between place and education in a way that has clear implications for both the scale of children's learning environments and the nature of the educational experiences in which they engage. A common rationale for introducing Internet technologies into classrooms is to enable students to learn more about other cultures through on-line interaction with peers around the world. With new technological innovations related to video conferencing and faster modem connections, students are now able to have face-to-face conversations with individuals all over the world.

The sanctity of place. The same technological innovations that have expanded children's learning environments also threaten to lessen their safety in schools. For the first time in the history of formal education, sexually explicit images, hate literature, and other inappropriate material are now readily accessible to children in school. (In the cyber age, censoring what children read in storybooks may well be a moot point.) On-line predators also have access to schoolchildren through the very on-line activities (e.g., Web browsing and chat) that teachers assign them to complete in class. Acceptable use policies, Web site blockers, and the ever watchful supervision of children's on-line activities by teachers can help to ease the danger, but these practices in themselves point to the changing landscape of the school as a place where children may no longer be safe from the dangers outside the school walls.

The place of children. Current and emerging high technologies have the potential to transform the idea and role of the child in society. Children now spend increasing amounts of their leisure time interacting with other children (and adults) on-line, and much of this (often unsupervised) time is spent in chat rooms and in on-line gaming environments. The lingo, social cues, rituals, and rules invented and practiced by children in these environments have the potential to forge a new on-line culture of childhood that is independent of the culture of childhood found (and, to a certain degree, regulated by adults) on city streets and playgrounds around the world. On a complementary basis, the technical competencies associated with harnessing Internet technologies in business have turned a select group of children and adolescents into business entrepreneurs. Teenagers have started profitable (sometimes very profitable) Web design firms and popular for-profit portal sites (Tapscott, 1998). A few others have successfully played the stock market by using the Internet to studiously research listed companies and manage on-line portfolios. Although these young entrepreneurs are few and far between, the widespread publicity they often receive is helping to forge a new view of the "economic child," an invented child who is on an equal footing with adults when it comes to competing in the private sector world.

PLACE AND PEDAGOGY IN THE CYBERSCHOOLING AGE

In wealthy countries all around the world, school districts have outfitted their educational facilities with the latest in computer hardware and software. School buildings are wired to support fast (sometime wireless) network and Internet connectivity between schools and around the world. Computer labs that can accommodate dozens of computer workstations are housed in dedicated classrooms. Project studios with cutting-edge peripherals—LCD projectors, color printers, scanners, stylus pens, CD/DVD burners, digital video cameras, synthesizers, scientific data-gathering tools, GIS software, robotics, and more—are integrated into traditional classrooms. Schools are embarking on ambitious laptop programs that equip all teachers and students with their own portable computers. School districts are actively partnering with the private sector, signing cofunding partnerships with high-tech companies, developing in-house software, and purchasing educational site licenses for commercial software. Report cards are being completed using "Webified" student tracking tools that allow parents to continuously monitor their child's progress. Students are producing live newscasts, multimedia presentations, charts, graphs, and reports that rely on the same downloaded scientific and geographical data used by professionals all over the world. Students are visiting, via cyberspace, ecoregions, landmarks, museums, and distant places around the world.

The above reforms in K–12 education serve as real-world examples of what is happening now in technology in education circles. However, these efforts may well pale in comparison to the kinds of place experiences afforded to future generations of children in the decades ahead.

In the not-too-distant future, a 10-year-old girl—let's call her Laura—wakes up one morning excitedly anticipating the coming day. It is 3 a.m. but Laura is oblivious to the darkness outside. Holographic windows in her bedroom make it seem like a bright sunny morning and, after all, she did retire early yesterday at 16:00 GMT. (GMT is now the agreed-upon standard for time all over the world.) Laura's first meeting of the day is with a 13-year-old pen pal halfway around the world. It is too late to wash and dress so, rather than connecting via real-time video conferencing, she instead chooses a 3D avatar from her digital character collection to appear at the meeting in place of herself. The avatar will perfectly translate all of Laura's facial expressions, verbal inflections, and body language without any effort on Laura's part. As Laura has (accidentally?) double booked another meeting for the same time, she assigns an intelligent avatar to represent her (with apologies) at this second meeting. This avatar has been given specific tasks to accomplish and questions to ask. It will report back to Laura, at her convenience, once the meeting has concluded. Now Laura is effectively in three places at once.

6:00: As she slept, Laura's computer was busy collating data for a research project she has negotiated with her teacher-mentor. (Laura's on-line mentor has 50 pupils in some 14 countries. Each is pursuing an interest-driven individual/collaborative learning plan of one's own design.) The data that her computer has collected, organized, reworded, and summarized is ready for presentation to Laura whenever she wants. Using a holographic white board, Laura pushes and pulls the textual, visual, and auditory data—*Minority Report* style—from one place to another until she is satisfied with its order, discarding what is not needed and privileging the most important. Laura knows that her teacher-mentor will evaluate her not on her ability to paraphrase and graphically "re-present" the content she has collected (her computer will handle this task with no problem), but on the originality of the synaptic bindings she forges, as she connects together seemingly disparate content categories to create new networked bindings not hosted on the Internet to date.

10:00: The "real world" is just now waking up and Laura has scheduled the daily physical R & R required by law for all children for the next 2 hours. (This law was enacted almost a decade before to guard against the muscular atrophy, obesity, and questionable psychological effects of total virtual immersion.) She participates in a timeless game of hide-and-seek with some local children at the playground some two blocks away from home.

12:00: In Laura's day, physical play and mealtimes are pretty much the only real-world activities that remain. Work, leisure, and learning are now all conducted on-line. Rarely is there the need for Laura or her parents to travel by air for business or pleasure, nor are there many (solar-powered) cars on the road, as almost all work is conducted from home. Ten-year-old Laura meets with friends at a local restaurant where she spends some of the pocket money she has made designing intelligent avatars for girls her own age through her small business.

13:30: Laura arrives home with plans to enter her family's "CAVE," a dedicated room in her house with full coverage holographic projection screens for walls, ceiling, and floor. From the menu of 50 places that her parents have leased, Laura chooses an asteroid adventure space to explore and map. As she moves through the space, the virtual "conveyor belt" for a floor underfoot moves backward, forward, and sideways, ensuring that Laura is always centered in the scene. The realism is just too tempting. Laura reaches out to grab some space dust that she has kicked up from the rocky surface below, but there is nothing to grab hold of. One day, Laura knows, holographic technology will have matured to the point where a child can grab hold of that space dust and slowly let it seep through her fingers, feeling the fine granular texture of each speck. How Laura wishes she were living 100 years in the future!

15:00: Laura has now been awake for 12 hours. Growing tired, she returns to her room and verbally instructs her computer to perform an "overnight" Internet search. She carefully lays down the search rules her computer should follow as it links to and collates the found content for a new subtopic her research project will address. As she slips under the covers, relaxing surround sound music fills the room and the holographic windows fade into a nighttime prairie scene. Laura claps her hands twice to turn off the lights :)

Chapter 6

THE PUBLIC AND THE PRIVATE

*Education lies at the intersection of two sets of competing rights. The first
is the right of parents to choose the experiences, influences, and values
to which they expose their children, the right to rear their children in
the manner that they see fit. The second is the right of a democratic
society to use the educational system as a means to reproduce its
most essential political, economic, and social institutions through
a common schooling experience.*
—Henry M. Levin (1991, p. 140)

Sporting something of a futuristic tone, the closing paragraphs of the previous chapter herald the potential impact of high technology on the future construction of place in education. In an indirect way, computers are now altering the *place of education in society*. Most school districts cannot afford to populate schools with high technology on their own and, even if they could, there are ongoing costs associated with hardware and software support/upgrading and teacher training that need to be funded each year. Given the current budgetary realities noted in Chapter 3, many schools are turning to private sources of funding and support. Schools throughout the United States and elsewhere in the world are forging technological alliances with high-tech suppliers such as Apple, IBM, and Microsoft. In addition, nontechnological firms such as fast-food companies are funding high-tech programs in exchange for in-school advertising and promotional opportunities.

The U.S. Department of Education estimated as early as 1996 that it would cost well over $100 billion over 10 years to carry out the federal government's plan to wire the nation's schools and support the new technological infrastructure though teacher inservicing, hardware maintenance, and software purchasing programs, among other expenses. (Contrast this with the 1994–1995 school year, in which U.S. schools spent about $3.3 billion on technology.) In reflecting on these numbers, the Department of Education concluded that only a partnership between

public education and the private sector could bring the cyberschooling
vision into fruition:

> The conclusion that leaps from these numbers is that schools alone cannot
> meet their need. It will take a partnership of the private sector, states and
> local communities, and the federal government to shoulder the financial
> burden of meeting these goals. Additionally, it will take careful planning to
> make certain that, in our reach for technological literacy, schools in all types
> of communities—middle income, lower-income, and better-off communities—
> have access to up-to-date technology in their classrooms. (p. 2)

What are the long-term consequences of an increasing reliance on
private-sector funding to support public education? Will public education
over time lose its autonomy in the face of corporatist interests? What impact
does in-school private-sector marketing have on the short- and long-term
purchasing decisions of students, and do such programs fly in the face of
media literacy programs that encourage students to be wary consumers?
Each of these questions point to the changing landscape of public education, a growing predicament in which public and private interests cannot
be readily distinguished from one another in schools:

> Schools trying to look and sound more like their prospective [private sec-
> tor] consorts still face stiff competition as they try to snag a particularly de-
> sirable corporate partner. A technology partnership broker, who refers to
> such arrangements as marriages, tells schools to be prepared to give up some
> decision-making autonomy and to allow business "to access students and
> teachers." He says even if companies are denied on-site advertising, they will
> still expect their contributions to pay dividends in increased sales. (Robertson,
> 1998, p. 283)

The move from public- to private-sector funding has significant implications for the idea of place in education. In light of the perceived need
to continually update the technological infrastructure of schools, the sanctity and autonomy of public education can no longer be assured. Private
interests, economic growth, brand loyalty, school choice, and marketing
ploys are increasingly the name of the educational funding game, and this
foci will likely continue to be felt in educational environments for years
to come. It will be felt on a physical level, through billboard advertisements,
sponsored curricula, and pop machines; on a virtual level, through corporate screen savers and Web banner advertisements; and on an ideological
level, as public and private interests do battle in forging the schools of
tomorrow. At issue is the very place and role of education in society for
the foreseeable future.

THE PROMISE AND PERIL OF PUBLIC EDUCATION

Public education in the United States, perhaps more than any other social institution, was born out of a faith in the public school to further the aims of the democratic citizenry that it was deemed to serve. The founding fathers placed the promise of the common school at the center of their hopes for a young fledging democracy. Thomas Jefferson lauded the potential for public education to inculcate the knowledge and skills required by a democratic citizenry intent on defending its right to govern constructively. Horace Mann's faith in the common school linked the need for a common democratic value system to the promise of social progress.

A number of social movements in the 19th and early 20th centuries expressed their own faith in the role of the public school in furthering the aims of a democratic society (Engel, 2000). Throughout the 1820s and 1830s, the Workingmen's parties promoted public education as a means of securing political equality. A century later, the rise of the labor and suffrage movements gave a prominent role to public education in furthering the aims of democratic egalitarianism for workers and women, respectively.

There has never been a truly democratic system of education—only a public system that has, at various times in its 200-year history, aspired to democratic ideals. Whether functioning as the social and political center of town life in the 1800s, serving as a coveted forum for the acquisition and practice of democratic skills and ideals early in the 20th century, or functioning as a corrective or compensatory measure to unchecked societal influences in the present age, the democratic potential of the school has always been tied to its enduring formal structure, universal accessibility, and common school origins.

Democracy and Education

In the early decades of the 20th century, during the heyday of the progressive education movement, John Dewey (1916/1966) articulated the democratic ideal for public education in a substantive way. Fundamental to Dewey's thinking was the notion of the democratic society as the basis for community life. For Dewey, the term "democracy" implied something more than a particular form of government. A truly democratic society comprised a "mode of associated living, a conjoint communicated experience" (Dewey, 1916/1966, p. 87) that fostered an experimental temperament within its citizenry and advocated community-based participatory approaches to decision making. The effectiveness of this type of social arrangement was largely dependent on a well-informed public with skills in critical decision-making and community building. Hence the need for an educational system that fostered skills in independent thinking and cooperative learning.

Underlying Dewey's conception of participative community life was his rejection of the primacy of the individual, autonomous in his or her functioning and independent of society. Dewey argued that the individual could only be fully conceived of and realized in relation to the larger society of which one was a part. Society was not simply a collection of detached individuals, each intent on securing from society the means for pursuing one's own private goals. Rather, the individual was an embodiment of his or her social relations, relations that Dewey privileged over the individual self-interest of the capitalistic conception of the individual.

Dewey's conception of "self" married elements of both the emerging fields of psychology and sociology, and it also introduced a temporal dimension that saw the individual and society developing in tandem with one another through time. For Dewey, the question of whether education should service the needs of the individual over society (or visa versa) was moot. Neither the individual nor society could be conceived of without referencing the other. The freedom of the individual could only be secured through the progressive application of social intelligence to the problems and decisions inherent to community life. Insofar as social intelligence could be judiciously practiced, the individual and society would remain conjoined, forming a dialectical relationship in an endless spiral of growth and development in the name of social, scientific, and technological progress.

Dewey's conception of place challenged the commonly held atomistic notion of a fixed and predetermined universe comprising a set of permanent values and static knowledge that could be transmitted piecemeal to each successive generation. Taking an opposite view, Dewey argued that humans live in an indeterminate world that undergoes constant change and flux. In Dewey's view, the world was made up of process, not product. (Indeed, process *was* product in the making.) The aim of education was to enrich this unfolding process of growth and development in a dialectical way that enriched both the individual and society.

The implications of such a view for a democratic system of education are significant. It is within the purpose of education to nurture in students the social intelligence and cognitive disposition required for active participation in community life. The participative and community-minded nature of democracy provides a rich and dynamic forum within which social values and practices can be continually renewed and reconstructed in light of the ever-changing social context. For children and adolescents, the public school serves as a coveted place and testing ground upon which the knowledge, skills, and values required for full participation in community life—

both in the here and now and later in adulthood—can be acquired and practiced.

Social Reconstructionism

Dewey was more a philosopher than a practitioner and although the progressive education movement successfully appropriated certain facets of his thought in the 1920s and 1930s, it misrepresented other important aspects of his work, particularly those aspects related to democratic education (Carr & Hartnett, 1996). Most importantly, in light of the above discussion, Dewey's qualified support for a child-centered approach to education was taken to an extreme by some progressive educators. They adopted a laissez-faire attitude to children's freedom in classrooms and favored the primacy of individual choice over Dewey's articulation of the social nature of the educational process. This misrepresentation of his ideas on education moved Dewey to sharply censure the progressive education movement and clarify the basic tenets of his democratic philosophy of education in 1938.

Dewey's criticisms of the extreme child-centered wing of the progressive education movement reflected the growing disillusionment of many educators who saw a fledging society beyond the fleeting wishes of the individual child and sought a more activist role for schools in shaping that society's democratic potential. During the early history of the progressive education movement, social reconstructionist thinkers led by George S. Counts (1932/1969) believed that schools should play an active role in transforming society. They seized on Dewey's notion of the school as a dynamic rather than reflexive agency and proposed a radical program of action for students. Working in sharp opposition to the social efficiency educators of the day (who attempted to make schools better serve the dictates of the labor market), social reconstructionists sought to use schools as vehicles for opposing unchecked capitalism, transforming culture and bringing a lagging society in line with the changing conditions of modern life.

Significantly, many child-centered educators did not share the social reconstructionists' view that the primary function of schools was to serve as a catalyst for social change. Rather, they believed that the expressed needs of the individual child should be the central focus of schools. This set up a dichotomy between the efforts of those progressive educators who argued that the progressive curriculum should be designed around the needs and interests of the individual child and those who argued that the curriculum should reflect the social and political problems of the day. With the rise in tensions between these two opposing visions in the 1930s and early 1940s came the gradual separation of the reconstructionist wing from the progressive education movement. With this separation, progressive education lost much of the political radicalism and social perceptiveness that defined its early history (temporarily regained in the 1960s and early 1970s) and gradually succumbed to the conservative forces of the day (Miller, 1997).

Dewey's critique of progressive education was an important early signal that public education would not be immune from criticism in the years ahead. That this early challenge came from the left of the political spectrum is a historical irony. In the decades to follow, progressive reforms in public education, some of which had the potential to deepen the democratic nature of the educational process, would also come under attack, but from quarters far less sympathetic than Dewey and the social reconstructionists.

Sputnik

Even before the Soviet Union launched the first orbiting satellite into space in October 1957, public schools were facing increased scrutiny from critics who charged that progressive education emphasized so-called nonacademic pursuits over the development of students' intellectual capacities. The launching of Sputnik introduced a new feeling of fear into the debate over the place of education in society and, for the next several years, firmly entrenched that debate within the context of the Cold War (Kliebard, 1987). For perhaps the first time in American history, it was events outside the United States that provided the impetus for educational reform. Critics charged that the United States was losing the battle for economic and military supremacy and the chief culprit responsible for this failure was the public school.

Over the course of the next decade and in the name of national security, new investments in mathematics and science education would be made by the federal government and calls for a new rigorous approach to teaching would gain favor. The place of education in society became firmly intertwined with concerns for U. S. national security and America's future economic and technological prowess.

Human Capital Theory

Insofar as it was a singular event, the launching of Sputnik, which contextualized much of the debate over the place of education in society in the late 1950s, the 1960s saw the gradual emergence of a newfound market ideology for education in the 1960s that has underlied much of the debate over the economics of education ever since.

Early formulations of human capital theory (Becker, 1964; Denison, 1963) extended the economic value traditionally ascribed to the material world to the labor force. Increases in productivity and personal income were equated with knowledge and skill investments in people. It was no longer sufficient to cite land, labor, and material capital as the sole harbingers of economic success. Rather, investments in human capital, in training and education, provided their own high rates of return, not only for those workers who were the direct recipients of training, but also for the wider economy more generally.

Far from playing a defensive role (as it did during the Sputnik era), education and training were now optimistically heralded as key to the labor force's social and economic development. New federal and state initiatives, including educational loans, antipoverty programs, and public relations campaigns promoted the place of education in improving the lives of both the privileged and disadvantaged. Educational researchers and economists produced studies that demonstrated clear linkages between educational investment and economic success. Human capital theory successfully married economics and education in a way that established a new empirical and quantitative justification for the place of education in supporting the market economy. Monies paid out to schools were no longer to be labeled as consumptive expenditures. Instead they were to be seen as educational investments in the future.

The rise of human capital theory had clear benefits for schools. It produced an outpouring of monetary investment in education and, just as importantly, gave public schools a privileged role to play in forging future economic and social progress. Yet, at the end of the day, this newfound economic view of schools was beholden to the principles of market ideology. In the view of democratic proponents, the purpose of education was myopically limited to fulfilling the needs of the market economy as measured exclusively through quantitative data that rationalized educational investments solely in terms of economic outcomes (Engel, 2000). If the economic rationale of monetary investments in education were ever to be questioned, public schools might well lose much of the public's esteem. Indeed, educators might even be put into the defensive position of having to justify monetary investments in public education solely on the basis of economic rates of return and using quantitative data alone (Chamberlain, 1971).

"A Nation at Risk"

It is precisely the above reversal of fortune that came to haunt the debate over public education in the 1980s. By 1980, the American economy was in decline. Having established a strong causal link between education and economic health in the previous 30 years, public schools were assigned much of the blame. The economic recession of the late 1970s and early 1980s gave rise to a number of scathing critiques of North American education. Beginning in 1984 with the publication of *A Nation at Risk*, numerous government and business reports (followed by many single-authored books in the 1990s and beyond) began calling for a "total overhaul" and "massive restructuring" of public education based on the charge that schools were failing to prepare young people adequately for the challenges of a competitive global marketplace. Typically subsumed within a discourse of crisis, these reports argued that only a drastic shift in the educational priorities of public schools could secure the economic future of the United States and ensure the future employability of students.

These reports were prompted by an increase in international economic competition and a perceived decline in the educational standards of schools and the basic literacy, numeracy, and thinking skills of students. They emerged out of a place context that saw the United States economy in transition, moving from a labor-intensive industrial economy to a technologically intensive and information-based postindustrial economy. That schools should respond to the changing conditions of the labor market had already been established by the proponents of human capital theory. What many of the business reports being produced in the 1980s argued for was a new planning agenda for public education that linked the school curriculum to shifts in demographic and employment trends. In short, schools should tailor their efforts to specific job categories, particularly those scientific, technical, and business-related vocations that would become ever more plentiful in an emerging postindustrial society. In the minds of most business executives, educational policy makers, as well as the general public, the first obligation of schools was to ensure the future employability of students.

In addition to a postindustrial focus, the place context of education in the 1980s went international. School critics pitted the American economy against its stiffest international competitors, particularly Japan and Germany. By closely attending to what these economically productive countries were doing right with their schools, educational policy makers could reorient the U.S. public school system to the needs of a growth economy and gradually turn trade deficit/surplus and productivity levels to America's advantage.

The internationalization of the place of education in society was taken one step further as educational critics linked their calls for reform to the often disappointing results of international achievement tests assessing the basic knowledge of students in a variety of subject areas (especially math and science). American students consistently performed below average on these tests and such poor results were linked to the failure of schools to teach basic literacy, numeracy, and problem-solving skills. Such conclusions were reinforced by calls for educational reform by employers and university instructors who argued that the public schools were sending them increasing numbers of illiterate students.

School Choice

Insofar as the 1980s served as a decade of discontent against the public school, the 1990s served as the decade in which many educational critics gave up on reform from within and began seeking outright alternatives to public education. Calls for the public funding of private schools and support for school choice initiatives such as home schooling, charter schools, and school vouchers increasingly gained favor. Such demands attracted much in the way of media attention throughout the decade and were backed up by plenty of pressure from market reform advocates. By 2001, 18 U.S. states supported some form of statewide school choice while another 19 offered limited school choice programs in specific school districts. In all, medium-to-strong charter school laws were in place in some 22 states, with pressures growing on other states to follow suit (Moffit et al., 2001).

At the heart of the school choice debate are two different, but not necessarily competing, notions of privacy. In the first view, there is the call for parental choice in education—the right of parents to send their children (and educational taxes) to the public or private school of their choice. In the second view, there is the call to bring market discipline to education, for schools to compete with each other just as businesses do in the private sector:

> Market advocates argue that, without competition, state schools have no incentive to satisfy the preferences of parents or to ensure that pupils achieve the highest educational attainment of which they are capable. . . . School monopolies, like any other, will be inefficient and will operate in the interests of providers, not customers. Only competitive pressure will induce schools to serve the interests of parents and children to the fullest extent possible. The same basic argument holds for competition between suppliers of school inputs. If the local . . . school district is the monopoly supplier, it has no incentive to be efficient. (Levacic, 2002, p. 32)

Whether or not privatization proposals for education are warranted or not is, of course, a matter of heated debate within educational circles. At the heart of this debate are competing visions of the place of education in a 21st century postindustrial democratic society. Does public education

deserve a privileged and protected place in society that is separate from
the market economy in which most other sectors of society compete?
Educational reform proposals related to charter schools, school vouchers,
public funding of private schools, and school choice more generally have
shaken the foundations (critics would say complacency) of public education by presenting a series of alternative futures for K–12 education in
which the democratic ideal of a common school experience that is shared
by all children does not figure.

CONTESTING THE PUBLIC PLACE OF EDUCATION IN SOCIETY

Not only is the sanctity of public education presently under threat, but
also perhaps are the very democratic ideals put forward by social vision-
aries such as Jefferson, Mann, and Dewey. National polls routinely demonstrate that faith and idealism in the potential of liberal democracy has
largely given way to political cynicism, apathy, and a loss of trust in
political leadership of all stripes. Massive (and oftentimes violent) pro-
tests by disaffected youth and social groups estranged from the democratic process routinely greet world leaders at G–8 summits and other
economic conferences. In the United States and, indeed, many other
countries around the world, political participation, including the most
basic act of voting every few years, is at an all-time low. On television,
most Americans are shielded from the workings of government and
exposed only to the political theater of party conventions, contested
(presidential) elections, and cursory political debate that is arguably more
soap opera than substance. That the tragedy of terrorist attacks on U.S.
soil has served to awaken Americans to the all-important role of government in securing this country's homeland defense there can be no doubt,
but it is not clear that this newfound reliance on government will translate into any greater political participation in those public policy issues
not directly related to national security.

America has, some might argue, evolved into a passive democracy, a
political system in which the wheels of government and, indeed, community, turn quite independently of the need for involved political participation by the average citizen who is, in turn, left to pursue his or her own
individual goals of personal and familial self-fulfillment. Whether wel-
comed by privacy proponents or not, this change in the relationship of the
individual to the public commons does underscore the arguments of those
who seek to introduce market discipline into education. In the eyes of many
privacy supporters, public education, at least as it is presently conceived,
has outlived its usefulness. In the increasingly globalized postindustrial

society of the 21st century, K–12 schools should better serve the interests of students who will soon be making their way in a competitive adult working world where merit and competition are the guiding principles upon which power, privilege, and prestige are awarded.

At the root of the market reform argument for education is a distrust in government which, save for a few essential services (e.g., defense and public works), is judged by privatization proponents to be split off from the interests of both freedom-loving individuals and the unfettered performance of a market economy. (Contrast this position with that of public school supporters, who are apt to see in participatory forms of government the core of the public commons they so value.) The perceived spiraling, out-of-control growth of government throughout the last century, its increasing intrusiveness in the daily lives of individuals, its failure to rise to the governance ideals of the founding fathers, its massive bureaucracy and taxation of individual wealth, its effort to regulate the redistribution of wealth from rich to poor, and its poor performance in providing the services it does control underlie the indictment of both government and public institutions more generally, including the public school (Murphy, 1996). Privatization proponents see in market reforms the discipline, rigor, and efficiencies that public institutions lack:

> The theoretical argument for privatization rests on a competitive model to demonstrate the efficiency of private production and a public choice government failure model wherein the public sector does too much and does it inefficiently. (Pack, 1991, p. 287)

> Competition works much better than [government] monopoly [and] a profit incentive is a stronger incentive than any bureaucratic management incentive. (Poole, 1985, p. 37)

Couple the above sentiments with both a more general shift to the right in U. S. politics and the increasing budgetary crises that many school districts face as they wrestle, for example, with the need to repair aging school facilities (Chapter 3) and upgrade the technological infrastructure of classrooms (Chapter 5). It may well be out of necessity that the lure of market reforms is increasingly gaining favor. That K–12 and postsecondary education are now seen as emerging markets that boast viable growth opportunities for the private sector only adds to the pressure to turn over to corporations the responsibility for running schools. The question that many public school advocates are asking is: Is the funding crisis in education "real" or manufactured by market reform advocates to bolster their case for privatization by establishing the necessary conditions for market reform in education (Robertson, 1998)?

COMMUNITY MINDEDNESS VERSUS INDIVIDUAL AUTONOMY

At the heart of the debate over public versus private interests in education is the notion of community. Public and private school proponents do
not simply hold competing views on community; rather, their educational
proposals extend from (and are beholden to) deep-seated and contrasting
cultural hypotheses concerning the roles of the individual and community in society.

Proponents of public education for a democratic citizenship begin with
a vision of the place of education in a society in which the public school
(and other democratic institutions) function at the core of the public commons, at the center of community life. It was noted earlier in this chapter
that Dewey regarded the individual and community as inseparable. Privileging one over the other was an oxymoron in his view, for each was a
reflection of the other. The same might well be said of participatory democracy. A truly democratic form of government does not function as an
entity external to the individual or community, nor should it be construed
as an intrusion on individual freedom. Quite the contrary, argue democratic proponents: A robust and stimulating democratic forum for public
discourse and policy-making reflects the pinnacle of social progress. Even
if we have not yet achieved this democratic ideal, it does not follow that
we should abandon this democratic project altogether (Carr & Hartnett,
1996). Doing so would further turn back the clock, weaken the public
commons, promote radical individualism at the expense of community collaboration, and substitute self-interest for wider social concern:

> Traditionally, the political world has offered a way to engage with others
> that is different from private life, a form of engagement known as democ-
> racy. The sense of empowerment that we gain whenever we become par-
> ticipants in the creation of our social and political world will be lost if we
> withdraw even further into our private lives or commercial dealings. (Frug,
> 1991, p. 308)

Public school supporters who laud the democratic purposes of education have always been at a disadvantage in the school reform debate.
Their ideological visions for public education represent something of a non-
quantifiable utopian ideal. Common school proponents pit their democratic
idealism against the real-world uncertainties of parents who worry about
their children's future economic security and (rightly or wrongly) see in
market reform proposals a pathway for addressing such concerns. Moreover,
the age-old democratic call for educational equality has not been realized
in practice. Educational investments in affluent and suburban public
school districts continue to outstrip those made in poor and urban school

centers (Kozol, 1991). More generally, we all live in an increasingly corporatist and materialistic world in which market reform proposals for education seem to extend naturally from our consumer personas. Each of these factors (and no doubt others) have made the democratic purposes of schooling argument the underdog in the debate over the place of education in society, particularly as those advocates propounding market ideology proposals have gained strength by successfully appropriating democratic and progressive reform rhetoric (Aronowitz & Giroux, 1993).

Consider this reminder, for example, that charter school reforms have the potential to problematize the public versus private school debate in education by creating a governance structure for schools that transcends the either/or debate between public and private school advocates:

> The charter school debate is polemicized between a model of market competition on [the] one hand and charges that charter reform is antidemocratic on the other. . . . Yet this polemic overlooks some key potentialities of charter reform in terms of democratic social reproduction. Charters are autonomous organizations within the public educational sphere that provide conditions for voluntaristic, associational school communities. . . . The voluntaristic and associational nature of charters raises the possibility that distinct schools may encourage a sense of belonging in students. A sense of belonging might provide a corrective to the widespread alienation that so often accompanies the contractual, bureaucratic relationship within traditional schools. Finally, the regulatory relief granted to charter schools raises the possibility that they might function as particularly democratic associations where public discourse surrounds common educational concerns and a spirit of civic participation is cultivated in both parents and students. (Smith, 2001, p. 175)

Do charter schools represent the compromise position between public and private school advocates? Can charter schools adequately preserve the common school experience that public school proponents seek to privilege while simultaneously infusing in schools the market discipline demanded of private school supporters? Or in competing for educational tax dollars, do for-profit private schools instead hold the key to quality education? Can public schools restore the public trust by charting a path that retains the common school experience while improving the quality of education for all? Whatever the answers to these critical questions, there are undoubtedly many fine examples of learning and teaching that go on in schools (public, charter, voucher-based, and private) every day. The above discussion is purely representative of the ideological context in which K–12 education is increasingly operating, and it is this wider ideational context that puts severe limits and pressures on the place of education in society, including the purpose of schools and the roles of students, teachers, and parents.

Consider, for a moment, the issue of educational accountability. Public schools in the United States and elsewhere around the world are increasingly operating in a competitive ethos in which the educational success of students, teachers, and schools is almost solely determined by comparative data extracted from student test scores using standardized tests alone. That this single-minded assessment approach is now so commonplace, taken-for-granted, and judged politically expedient is a testament not to the effectiveness of standardized tests, critics charge (Aronowitz & Giroux, 1993), but rather to the ubiquitous success of the advocates of such tests in limiting the debate over the place of education in society to a set of ideological principles directly derived from market ideology: namely, the primacy of the individual, the integrity of quantitative data, and the efficiency of market accountability.

PATHWAYS, BOUNDARIES, AND OTHER PLACE METAPHORS

It is clear from the above discussion that the K–12 school, perhaps more than any other social institution, does not exist solely unto itself, responding only to the expressed wishes of the students, teachers, and staff who enter and leave the school daily. A school receives much of its direction—indeed, pressure—from outside its four walls. This direction is multifaceted and, in many ways, place bound. Place concepts such as proximity, vantage point, pathways, scale, and boundaries are all at play in the debate over the place of education in society.

Proximity and vantage point. Various stakeholders (the term "stakeholder" is itself contentious among stakeholders) experience the place of education in society on different scales and from unique vantage points. Some stakeholders, most notably students and teachers, inhabit schools for 6 or more hours a day. Their experience of the place of education in society is direct and intimate, so it is perhaps not surprising that some students and teachers may at times resent the pressures placed on schools by those who are perceived to be "outside" the institution. Other stakeholders, such as parents, have no less a vested interested in what goes on in schools but, far from inhabiting school, they experience the school as a place from afar. Most parents are dependent on daily, if often cursory, accounts from their children. (Indeed, the very act of entering a school, perhaps to clear up a child's account of what is happening in school, can be intimidating for many parents.) Other stakeholders, such as employers and university faculty, may be even further removed from the school. Far from being concrete, their experience of the place of education in society is very nearly an abstraction, an amalgamation of personal, professional, and public views, but they nevertheless express an expectation of something to be fulfilled in the public space of the school in terms of the quality of graduates that are sent on to them. Young children, first-year high school students, older students nearing graduation, teachers, administrative staff, parents, employers, educational researchers, and the general public all have a potentially unique vantage point from which to view the place of education in society and, indeed, this vantage point changes throughout our lives as we first enter school as a young child, graduate as a young adult, send our own children to school years later, and potentially enter our twilight years without any direct connection to public education.

Positioning. Taking the above point a step farther, the place of education in society is often defined in terms of the school's relationship to the various institutions and social/economic sectors represented by the above and other stakeholder groups: peers, teachers' federations, the family, the business world, and colleges and universities, among others. Representatives of these groups do not simply express an ideological viewpoint concerning the role of the school in society; rather, they seek to position the school in relationship to other social institutions and sectors of society— to put the school in its proper place, so to speak—as an institution that effectively responds to the expectations of parent groups, instills the job skills required by employers, and/or imparts the critical literacy skills required for higher education, and so on. The act of positioning schools relative to other social institutions implies that the place of education in society always exists in relationship, that schools are not social institutions that can be disconnected from (or pitted against) the rest of the world. That the school should not only exist in relationship, but also support or even serve other social institutions is a point upon which almost everyone— save those calling for a reconstructive role for education—agrees.

Pathways. As students navigate their way through the school system, they are presented with multiple pathways that are laden with both values and varying levels of future promise: urban versus suburban schools, segregated versus desegregated schools, mainstream versus special education classes, and academic versus (so-called) nonacademic instructional streams. Each have the potential to lead students to a variety of peer group, employment, and higher education destinations. Some pathways, such as the choice of secondary school and instructional stream, are often left to graduating elementary school students and their parents to ponder. Other pathways are pursued on the advice of specialists (e.g., special education) or constrained by the geographical location of a student's home address (e.g., a poorly performing school's catchment area). In the history of American education, there has been much debate over the ways in which educational pathways discriminate between students (e.g., African American and Hispanic children) and offer graduates varying levels of future prospects. (Indeed, at the time of this writing, the effort to mitigate the geostructural inequities between high and poor performing schools is a centerpiece of the Bush administration's rationale for the "No Child Left Behind" strategy.) That such a debate has at times been vigorous should not be surprising from a place perspective, for just as in the physical world of neighborhoods, play spaces, and home, varying levels of environmental quality in schools lead also to varying levels of privilege, promise, and potential in adulthood.

Scale. The importance of scale to the pedagogy of place was discussed in Chapter 2. Beyond the issue of how place should be taught, however, lies competing interests in whom should create and control the school curriculum: the state, the school district, or the individual classroom teacher. Supporters of local control of subject content cite the benefits of a decentralized curriculum that is responsive to the unique attributes and needs of the local community. From an opposite point of view, a state-mandated curriculum has the advantage of uniformity in subject content across multiple school districts. In the United States, there is also the well-publicized tension between the U. S. Department of Education and individual school districts, the latter which sees needed federal dollars tied to demonstratable improvements in student achievement. Control over budgets and curriculum are fought for at a variety of levels, including the federal, state, school district, and individual teacher.

Boundaries. If the centuries-old debate over public education could be reduced to just one question, it might well be this: What *is* and *is not* within the mandate of schools to teach? Every educational philosophy forwards a mandate for schools. This mandate articulates an underlying rationale for the curriculum under study and sanctions a particular methodology and approach to teaching. It provides answers to questions related to the purpose of education, the role of the school in society, and our obligations to future generations. It further makes clear the roles to be fulfilled by teacher and student, indicates what aspects of a student's life are within the pervue of the school or learning situation, and (often subtly) dictates whose values will dominate the educational process itself. Within a given educational philosophy, certain instructional content is privileged. Other content is categorically excluded (or tacitly excluded by omission). Should schools focus solely on the 3 Rs? Should they focus on the psychosocial needs of children? Should schools promote individual excellence and encourage a competitive spirit among students? Should they instead foster collaborative and cooperative learning among peers? Should schools teach values? Should they teach media literacy? Should schools promote critical thinking skills and, if so, should they do so within a social activist framework? The answers to each of these questions (and no doubt many others) together define the boundaries of what various stakeholders believe should and should not be happening in schools.

Business leaders and industry groups offer up their prescriptions for what is ailing schools. State departments of education issue new policy and reform mandates to school districts. Educational researchers propound new school improvement strategies. Parental advocacy groups put out their annual report cards on schools. Permeating the prescriptions for education offered up by these and other stakeholder groups is the distilling and editorial roles played by the media, which serves as the pivotal battleground upon which the debate over the place of education in society is played out.

Conclusion

THE LOSS OF PLACE IN EDUCATION?

*When shall we realize that in every school building in the land a struggle
is ... being waged against all that hems in and distorts human life? ...
In its slow and imperceptible processes, the real battles for human freedom
and for the pushing back of the boundaries that restrict human life
are ultimately won.*
—John Dewey (1930/1981, pp. 297–298)

This book has painted a picture of educational places in which the developmental, architectural, and philosophical play out an interwoven dialectic in schools and communities. For the infant and young child, place is first experienced on a deeply personal, intimate and sensorial level as the young child ever so tentatively places oneself in relationship to the matrices of caregiver, crib, home, and neighborhood in infancy and early childhood. From ages 6 to 12, the child forges a deeply felt sense of place (sometimes alone, other times with peers) as the boundaries of her play and learning spaces expand outward to include the wider (and sometimes unsupervised) community of neighborhood and school. Without adult direction, groups of children learn to mediate their play spaces all on their own. So, too, children begin, in concert with the influence of peers, adults, and popular culture, to ascribe meaning to distant, large-scale, and abstract places that they may never know firsthand. Finding one's place in the wider world also remains within the task of adolescence as teens experiment with membership in cliques, try out a variety of work roles, and take their first tentative steps (both figuratively and literally) in forging an independent place of their own. Throughout most of these formative years, the school functions as the sole formal means by which place, including geographic knowledge, mapping skills, and a sense of nationhood, can be explicitly taught to children. Schools compete with less formal institutions and influences, such as the peer group and popular culture, to provide a corrective or compensatory measure to children's developing sense of place.

Yet just as children give meaning to places, so do places give meaning to them. Both children and adults inhabit place. Spaces are imbued with meanings that are sometimes personal, but very often shared. Embedded in schools are a diversity of levels of environmental quality and functionality that underscore both the uniqueness of *my* school and its standing in comparison to others. Inside the school itself, some spaces (e.g., a student's locker) are carefully safeguarded private domains, while other spaces (e.g., the cafeteria) function as complex nested public spaces. Still other spaces (e.g., the staff room) are off limits to students or approached with an appropriate level of trepidation (e.g., the principal's office). Some spaces (e.g., the science lab) offer specialized design elements related to their unique function within the school, while other spaces (e.g., the typical classroom) aim for ubiquity in terms of the multiple uses to which they can be put.

For its part, the traditional classroom functions as a complex nested space within the school. It houses, for 6 or more hours each weekday, a modestly sized community of learners and a teacher. Signage on the classroom bulletin boards provide direction (and encouragement) to students. Individual desks provide housing. The carpeted area in an early primary classroom provides a communal meeting space that aims to convey a homey feel. Pathways and aisles provide efficient routes into, out of, and through the learning setting. Some classrooms sport a traditional "desks in rows" arrangement that supports a direct instruction approach to teaching. In other classrooms, student desks are purposefully arranged into groups or removed altogether in favor of a centers-based approach. Embedded in each of these and many other classroom designs is an ideological vantage point that proscribes and directs the arrangement and use of classroom space to serve a particular pedagogical philosophy.

Although they may learn, teach, work, and otherwise reside in schools, those who daily inhabit schools are not the only ones who ascribe meaning to places in education. Parents, employers, university faculty, and the wider public more generally also voice a variety of viewpoints when it comes to the place of education in society. Expectations for schools are pulled this way and that as various stakeholders and policy groups espousing competing views on education do battle in forging, at an ideological level, the schools of tomorrow.

In forging tomorrow's schools, educational reformers would be wise to heed the lessons of place in education lest the sanctity of K–12 schools as valued and protected places in society be undermined through direct challenge or outright neglect. Although geography proficiency in U. S. schools is showing modest signs of improvement (NCES, 2002), we need only step back to look at place through a slightly wider lens to reveal worrying signs of an uncertain path ahead for the experience of place in education. The deepening school infrastructure crisis (Chapter 3), the resegregation of American schools (Orfield & Eaton, 2003), threats to homeland security ("Schools Mull," 2003), the ever pervasive forces of globalization (O'Sullivan, 1999; Spring, 1998) and calls to deschool, privatize, and/or "cyberfy" education (Chapters 5 and 6) all have the potential to transform the experience of place in education in the coming years.

Celebrating place. In the face of such challenges, how can educators strengthen a sense of place in education? One important taken-for-granted strategy is already evident in many schools today in the form of school spirit. Schools that are embued with a strong sense of spirit are more apt than others to evoke a strong commitment to place on the part of students and faculty. Keeping a school clean, safe, and free from bullying are surely critical starting points (as is naming a school, rather than merely assigning it a number), but how well a school measures up to other area schools (particularly in terms of academic and athletic successes) can also deepen a sense of pride in place for both students and staff. At key moments throughout the year, students celebrate their accomplishments in the form of concerts, school plays, and graduation ceremonies (similar to the vignette that opened Chapter 1). Younger students adorn the walls of their elementary school with completed artwork. A secondary school's awards cabinet proudly celebrates the historical legacy of the school through plaques and trophies attesting to the academic and athletic prowess of the school's alumni (see Figure 7.1).

Celebrating metaphors of place. Embedded in some philosophies of education are classroom metaphors of place. Nancy Atwell's (1998) vision of a whole language classroom, for example, weaves the metaphor of a writer's publishing house complete with peer editors, bookbinders, and writers' circles. In another classroom, when it's time for fourth-grade science period, the teacher asks her students to don their lab coats. For the duration of the science period, students are refered to as "Dr." Still other teachers turn their classrooms into small-scale cities for a community studies unit. Students use the classroom space to build up a city, take on a diversity of community roles, produce a community newspaper, shop, run for office, and operate local businesses. In each of these examples, there is a classroom metaphor at work, a metaphor that transcends the traditionally agreed upon boundaries of what a classroom should be.

Studying a diversity of places. From the microworlds of amoebas to the numinous universe beyond our solar system, the pedagogy of place offers a diversity of levels and contexts within which to learn. Place study offers teachers the opportunity to infuse a sense of wonder and magic into teaching, to excite children's imaginations through flights of fantasy (and reality)

FIGURE 7.1. The entryway to many schools celebrates the academic and athletic accomplishments of the school's alumni. Visitors are reminded of the historic legacy of the school as home to successive generations of students.

evoked through storybooks, guided imagery, treasure maps, microscopes, and so on. Soo, too, the study of faraway and long-ago places offers older students a window into the historical legacy of cultures and societies (e.g., Ancient Egypt) that have contributed so much to the here-and-now places that today embed our lives. From a complementary perspective, the study of esoteric places can bring to the fore unreflected-upon assumptions about the immediate, seemingly mundane and taken-for-granted places that remain unexamined in students' own lives.

Attending to place. Many of those taken-for-granted places exist within and around the school itself (Butchart, 1986). As a starting point for the study of place, the interior and exterior of the school can serve as an immediately accessible site for students' mapping and measurement activities, space usage analyses, and media literacy studies related to signage, wayfinding, et cetera.

Inviting students and their parents to return to the school playground at night to participate in some stargazing can transform the taken-for-granted daylight experience of school through a magical, never-to-be-forgotten nighttime lesson in astronomy. So, too, in many built-up urban communities, stepping just outside of the school to take students on a walking tour of the local community can effectively revive a long-neglected topic area within social studies—namely, architecture—by integrating the study of local history, historical and contempoary building design, the visual arts, and mathematics, among other subjects (Olsen & Olsen, 2001).

Problematizing the virtual. When it comes to field trips and experiential learning, many educators and parents remain suspicious of calls to cyberfy education, to supplant learning in the "real world" with on-line experiences conducted over the Internet. It is not solely a question of protecting the sanctity of the real world (i.e., the natural and built environments), itself a laudable goal from a place perspective. Technological critics also raise developmental concerns related to the seemingly ever increasing attachment of children to computer technology, often beginning in early childhood (Armstrong & Casement, 1998). Piaget (1973), Montessori (1995), and developmental psychologists more generally remind us that it is the interaction of hand, eye, and brain with *concrete* objects in the physical world which propels cognitive development to new levels of understanding throughout infancy, and early and middle childhood. That interactive technologies (e.g., gloves and "CAVES") might one day match or surpass the "inputs" that young children now receive via the physical world is a dubious, even ominous, prospect for those who fear the ever-growing entrancement of children by computers, television, and video games. Yet as a defense against cyberschooling, sticking to direct instruction and textbook learning is very likely a poor strategy. Rather, it is absorbed immersion into rich multisensory environments based in the physical world of the built and natural environments that stands the best chance of forestalling the deschooling and cyberfying of society that some see as inevitable.

Heeding developmental experience. It was noted in the first chapter that as social institutions dedicated to the education of the young, schools are unique in their intergenerational makeup. Elementary school teachers and the young children they teach attend to and make sense of place in different ways. Although most philosophies of education choose by ommision to ignore developmental cues in how place might best be taught (Chapter 2) and classrooms designed (Chapter 4), attending to the rich diversity of children's place experiences can nevertheless enrich learning and build congruency between developmental psychology, the design of classroom space, and the pedagogy of place. To do so, however, requires that educators and school designers consciously "tune into" the ways in which children perceive space and construct mental maps as they mature. A renewed alliance between educational philosophy and the insights of developmental theory (an alliance originally forged almost a century ago by the promise of progressive reform, but largely overshadowed in recent years by the restricted notion of teaching as technique) could once again bring children's experiences of place into the fore in schools.

Children as designers. There is one additional way that educators can honor children's developmental experience of place—by inviting them to participate in the design process for new schools, classrooms, playgrounds, and other spaces in which children have a stake (see Figure 7.2). In many

FIGURE 7.2. The study of place can provide children with the opportunity to explore the concept of home as they design and build their very own dwelling, as in this example built by fourth-grade students.

ways, these places belong as much to children as they do to adults. Both children and adults inhabit, play, and learn in these spaces. If the classroom is a community and adults and children alike construct at an ideational level the places they inhabit, should children not be invited to participate, at more than a lip-service level, in the design and layout of the classrooms they inhabit for 6 or more hours each day? To honor the natural history of place in education is to honor *all* those who have a stake in the place of education in society as we forge the school buildings, learning settings, and place pedagogies of the future.

REFERENCES

Altman, I., & Chemers, M. (1980). *Culture and environment*. Monterey, CA: Brooks/ Cole Publishing.

Altman, I., & Werner, C. M. (Eds.). (1985). *Home environments*. New York: Plenum Press.

American Association of School Administrators. (1991). *Schoolhouse in the red*. Roslyn, VA: Author.

Archibugi, F. (1997). *The ecological city and the city effect: Essays on the urban planning requirements for the sustainable city*. Aldershot, UK: Ashgate.

Armstrong, A., & Casement, C. (1998). *The child and the machine: Why computers may put our children's education at risk*. Toronto: Key Porter Books.

Aronowitz, S., & Giroux, H. A. (1993). *Education still under seige*. Toronto: OISE Press.

Atkinson, C. (1938). *Education by radio in American schools*. Nashville: George Peabody College for Teachers.

Atwell, N. (1998). *In the middle: Writing, reading, and learning with adolescents*. (2nd ed.). Portsmouth, NH: Boynton/Cook.

Becker, G. (1964). *Human capital*. New York: Columbia University Press.

Bell, A. C. (2001). *Grounds for learning: Stories and insights from six Canadian school ground naturalization initiatives*. Toronto: Evergreen Foundation.

Bennett, N. et al. (1980). *Open plan schools: Teaching, curriculum, design*. Englewood, NJ: Humanities Press.

Bengtsson, A. (1972). *Adventure playgrounds*. New York: Praeger Publishers.

Black, S. (2001, October). Building blocks: How schools are designed and constructed affects how students learn. *American School Board*, [Available online]. http//www.asbj.com/lbd/2001/inprint/Black.html. Accessed on November 12, 2003.

Blitz, B. (1973). *The open classroom: Making it work*. Boston: Allyn & Bacon.

Bowers, C. A. (1995). *Educating for an ecologically sustainable culture: Rethinking moral education, creativity, intelligence, and other modern orthodoxies*. Albany: State University of New York Press.

Bowers, C. A. (2000). *Let them eat data: How computers affect education, cultural diversity, and the prospects for ecological sustainability*. Athens: University of Georgia Press.

Bradley, W. (1998). *Expecting the most from school design*. Charlottesville: Thomas Jefferson Center for Educational Design, University of Virginia.

153

Bronfenbrenner, U. (1979). *The ecology of human development: Experiments by nature and design.* Cambridge, MA: Harvard University Press.

Brubaker, C. W. (1998). *Planning and designing schools.* New York: McGraw-Hill.

Buck, G. (1994). Schools ways [Book review]. *Alberta Journal of Educational Research, XL*(1), 95–99.

Buehrer, E. (1990). *The new age masquerade.* Brentwood, TN: Wolgemuth & Hyatt.

Butchart, R. E. (1986). *Local schools: Exploring their history.* Nashville: American Association for State and Local History.

Carlgren, F. (1976). *Education towards freedom: Rudolf Steiner education and a survey of the work of Waldorf schools throughout the world.* East Grinstead, UK: Lanthorn Press.

Carr, W., & Hartnett, A. (1996). *Education and the struggle for democracy: The politics of educational ideas.* Buckingham, UK: Open University Press.

Casey, E. S. (1997). *The fate of place: A philosophical history.* Berkley: University of California Press.

Castaldi, B. (1987). *Educational facilities: Planning, modernization, and management.* Boston: Allyn & Bacon.

Center for Ecoliteracy. (1999). *The edible schoolyard.* Berkeley, CA: Learning in the Real World.

Center for the Prevention of School Violence. (1997). *How to establish and maintain secure, safe, and orderly schools.* Raleigh, NC: Center for the Prevention of School Violence.

Chamberlain, N. W. (1971). Some second thoughts on the concept of human capital. In R. A. Wykstra, *Human capital formation and manpower development.* New York: Free Press.

Clinton, W. J. (1996, November 12). *Public School Infrastructure.* Speech given at White House, Washington, D.C.

Coffey, A. (1996). Transforming school grounds. *Green Teacher, 47,* 7–10.

Counts, G. S. (1969). *Dare the school build a new social order?* New York: Arno Press. (Original work published 1932)

Cook, H. (1996). The new math of school design. *Building Design and Construction, 37*(8), 36–39.

Crowe, T. D. (1991). Safer schools by design. *Security Management, 35*(9), 81–84.

Cuban, L. (1986). *Teachers and machines: The classroom use of technology since 1920.* New York: Teachers College Press.

Darrow, B. (1932). *Radio: The assistant teacher.* Columbus, OH: R. G. Adams.

DeBlij, H. J. (2002). *Geography: Realms, regions, and concepts.* New York: John Wiley & Sons.

DeJesus, R. (1987). *Design guidelines for Montessori schools.* Milwaukee: Center for Architecture and Urban Planning Research, University of Wisconsin.

Denison, E. (1963). Measuring the contribution of education to economic growth. In Study Group in the Economics of Education (Ed.), *The residual factor and economic growth* (pp. 122–143). Paris: Organization for Economic Cooperation and Development.

Dewey, J. (1966). *Democracy and education.* New York: Free Press. (Original Work published 1916)

Dewey, J. (1981). Philosophy and education. In J. A. Boydston (Ed.), *John Dewey: The later works (1925–1953)* (Volume 5). Carbondale, IL: South Illinois University Press. (Original work published 1930)

Dewey, J. (1963). *Experience and education.* New York: Macmillan. (Original work published 1938)

Dovey, K. (1985). Home and homelessness. In I. Altman & C. M. Werner (Eds.), *Home environments* (pp. 65–86). New York: Plenum Press.

Dudek, M. (2000a). *Architecture of schools: The new learning environments.* Boston: Architectural Press.

Dudek, M. (2000b). *Kindergarten architecture: Spaces for the imagination* (2nd Ed.). London: Spon Press.

Duke, D. L. (1998). Challenges of designing the next generation of America's schools. *Phi Delta Kappan, 79*(9), 688–693.

Edison, T. (1922). As quoted in Cuban, L. (1986). *Teachers and machines: The classroom use of technology since 1920.* New York: Teachers College Press.

Education Writers Association. (1989). *Wolves at the schoolhouse door.* Washington, DC: Author.

Engel, M. (2000). *The struggle for control of public education: Market ideology vs. democratic values.* Philadelphia: Temple University Press.

Evergreen Foundation. (1994). *Welcoming back the wilderness: A guide to school ground naturalization.* Toronto: Prentice-Hall.

Food Works. (1992). *The Common Roots program.* Montpelier, VT: Author.

Ford Foundation. (1961). *Teaching by television.* New York: Author.

Frazier, L. M. (1993). *Deteriorating school facilities and student learning.* Eugene, OR: ERIC Clearinghouse on Educational Management. (ERIC No. ED356564.) [Available online]. http://www.ericfacility.net/ericdigests/ed356564.html.

Freire, P. (1984). *Pedagogy of the oppressed.* New York: Continuum.

Froebel, F. (1912). *Froebel's chief writings on education.* New York: Longman. (Original work published 1826)

Frug, J. (1991). The choice between privatization and publicization. In R. L. Kemp (Ed.), *Privitization: The provision of public services by the private sector* (pp. 305–310). Jefferson, NC: McFarland.

Gaddy, B. et al. (1996). *School wars: Resolving our conflicts over religion and values.* San Francisco: Jossey-Bass.

Gardner, H. (1991). *The unschooled mind: How children think and how schools should teach.* New York: Basic Books.

Gardner, H. (1999). *The disciplined mind: What all students should understand.* New York: Simon & Schuster.

Graves, B. E. (1993). *School ways: The planning and design of America's schools.* New York: McGraw-Hill.

Groat, L. (Ed.). (1995). *Giving places meaning.* London: Academic Press.

Gump, R., & Ross, F. (1979). Cited in Sanoff, H. (1994). *School design.* New York: Van Nostrand Reinhold.

Hainstock, E. G. (1986). *The essential Montessori.* New York: New American Library.

Harmon, A. (1998, August 30). Sad, lonely world discovered in cuberspace. *New York Times.*

Hart, R. (1979). *Children's experience of place*. New York: Irvington.

Harvey, M. (1989). Children's experiences with vegetation. *Children's Environments Quarterly, 6*(1), 36–43.

Harwood, A. C. (1958). *The recovery of man in childhood*. London: Hodder & Stoughton.

Heafford, M. R. (1967). *Pestalozzi: His thought and its relevance today*. London: Methuen & Co.

Hebert, E. (1992). Crow Island: A place built for children. In E. Hebert & A. Meek (Eds.), *Children, learning, and school design* (pp. 33–38). Winnetka, IL: Winnetka Public Schools.

Hird, A. (2000). *Learning from cyber-savvy students: How Internet-age kids impact classroom teaching*. Sterling, VA: Stylus.

Hirsch, E. D. (1987). *Cultural literacy: What every American needs to know*. New York: Vintage Books.

Holt, J. (1969). *The underachieving school*. New York: Dell Publishing.

Husserl, E. (1962). *Recherches logiques*. Paris: Presses Universitaires de France.

Hutchison, D. (1998). *Growing up green: Education for ecological renewal*. New York: Teachers College Press.

Hutchison, D. (1999). *School ground naturalization*. Toronto: Evergreen Foundation Archives.

Hutchison, D. (2003). Teaching nature: From philosophy to practice. *North American Montessori Teachers Association Journal, 28*(1), 207–218.

Jacobs, R. (1998, March 31). Year-round school helps space crunch. *San Jose Mecury News*.

Kallett, T. (1995). As quoted in Sobel, D. (1998). *Mapmaking with children: Sense of place education for the elementary years*. New York: Heinemann.

Kincheloe, Joe L. (2001). *Getting beyond the facts: Teaching social studies/social sciences in the twenty-first century*. New York: Peter Lang.

Kjos, B. (1990). *Your child and the new age*. Wheaton, IL: Victor Books.

Kliebard, H. M. (1987). *The struggle for the American curriculum, 1893–1958*. New York: Routledge & Kegan Paul.

Kolb, D. A. (1984). *Experiential learning: Experience as the source of learning and development*. Englewood Cliffs, NJ: Prentice-Hall.

Korosec-Serfaty, P. (1985). Experience and use of dwelling. In I. Altman & C. M. Werner (Eds.), *Home environments* (pp. 65–86). New York: Plenum Press.

Kowalski, T. J. (1989). *Planning and managing school facilities*. New York: Praeger.

Kozol, J. (1991). *Savage inequalities: Children in America's schools*. New York: Crown Publications.

Kraut, R. et al. (1998). Internet paradox: A social technology that reduces social involvement and psychological well-being? *American Psychologist, 53*(9), 1017–1031.

Lackney, J. A. (1994). *Educational facilities: The impact and role of the physical environment of the school on teaching*. Milwaukee: Center for Architecture and Urban Planning Research, University of Wisconsin-Milwaukee.

Lankshear, C. (1982). *Freedom and education: Toward a non-rationalist philosophy of education*. Auckland, New Zealand: Milton Brookes.

Levacic, R. (2002). School competition in England: A decade of experience. *Education Canada*, *42*(3), 32–35.

Levin, Henry M. (1991). The economics of educational choice. *Economics of Education Review*, *10*(2), 137–158.

Lewis, C. D. (1937). *The rural community and its schools*. New York: American Book.

Lewis, L. et al. (2001). *Condition of America's public school facilities: 1999*. Washington, DC: National Center for Education Statistics.

Lillard, P. P. (1973). *Montessori: A modern approach*. New York: Shocken Books.

Lillard, P. P. (1996). *Montessori today: A comprehensive approach to education from birth to adulthood*. New York: Schocken Books.

Lockridge, R. (1998, April 24). This school has top security. [Television broadcast]. *CNNin*.

Loughlin, C. E., & Suina, J. H. (1982). *The learning environment: An instructional strategy*. New York: Teachers College Press.

Lyndon, D. (1986). Caring about places: Recognition. *Places*, *4*(1), 2.

Lyons, J. B. (2002). The learning environment: Do school facilities really affect a child's education? In National Center for Educational Statistics. *Learning by Design 2002: A school leader's guide to architectural services*. Washington, DC: U. S. Department of Education.

MacKenzie, D. G. (1989). *Planning educational facilities*. New York: University Press of America.

Matthews, M. H. (1992). *Making sense of place: Children's understanding of large-scale environments*. Hemel Hempstead, UK: Harvester Wheatsheaf.

McCain, C. H. (1996). *Plugged in and turned on: Planning, coordinating, and managing computer-supported instruction*. Thousand Oaks, CA: Corwin Press.

McLaren, P. (1989). *Life in schools: An introduction to critical pedagogy in the foundations of education*. Toronto: Irwin Publishing.

Mendels, P. (1998a, March 18). Schools may get computers, but can they afford to keep them? *New York Times*, p. B10.

Mendels, P. (1998b, June 17). Schools, libraries cope with cuts in funding for Internet plan. *New York Times*, p. B10.

Merleau-Ponty, M. (1967). *Phenomenology of perception*. London: Routledge & Kegan Paul.

Miller, J. P. , & Seller, W. (1990). *Curriculum: Perspectives and practice*. Toronto: Copp, Clark, Pitman Ltd.

Miller, R. (1997). *What are schools for? Holistic education in American culture*. (3rd ed.). Brandon, VT: Holistic Education Press.

Mitchell, W. J. (1999). Foreword: Who put the space in cyberspace? In Peter Anders, *Envisioning cyberspace: Designing 3D electronic spaces*. New York: McGraw-Hill.

Moffit, R. E. et al. (2001). *School choice 2001: What's happening in the States*. Washington, DC: Heritage Foundation.

Montessori, M. (1963). *The secret of childhood*. Bombay: Orient Longmans. (Original work published 1936)

Montessori, M. (1995). *The absorbent mind*. New York: Henry Holt.

Moore, R. C. (1989). *Before and after asphalt: Diversity as an ecological measure of quality in children's outdoor environments.* In M. N. Bloch & A. Pellegrini (Eds.), *The ecological context of children's play* (pp. 191–213). Norwood, NJ: Ablex Publishing.

Moore, R. C., & Wong, H. H. (1997). *Natural learning: The life history of an environmental schoolyard.* Berkeley: MIG Communications.

Muller, R. (1989). A world core curriculum. *Social Education, 53*(5), 284–286.

Murphy, J. (1996). *The privatization of schooling: Problems and possibilites.* Thousand Oaks, CA: Corwin.

Napier-Anderson, L. (1988). *Change: One step at a time.* Toronto: OISE Press.

National Center for Education Statistics. (2001). *The Condition of Education.* Washington, DC: Author.

National Center for Education Statistics (NCES). (2002). *National assessment of education progress: The nation's report card.* Washington, DC: Author.

National Commission on Excellence in Education. (1984). *A nation at risk.* Cambridge, MA: USA Research.

National Governors Association. (1991). *Results in education, 1991.* Washington, DC: Author.

Neatby, H. (1953). *So little for the mind.* Toronto: Clarke, Irwin, & Company.

Neill, A. S. (1960). *Summerhill: A radical approach to child rearing.* New York: Hart.

NetDay. (2003). [Available online]. http://www.netday.org. Accessed on November 14, 2003

Norberg-Schulz, C. (1980). *Genius loci: Towards a phenomenology of architecture.* New York: Rizzoli.

Norberg-Schulz, C. (2000). *Architecture: Presence, language, place.* Milan, Italy: Skira.

Olsen, M. R., & Olsen, G. (2001). *Archi-techer: A Guide to architecture in the schools.* Champaign, IL: Olsen & Associates.

Ontario Ministry of Education and Training. (1998). *The Ontario curriculum: Social studies history and geography.* Toronto: Ontario Ministry of Education & Training.

Orfield, G., & Eaton, S. E. (2003, March 3). Back to segregation. *The Nation.*

Orr, D. (1992). *Ecological literacy: Education and the transition to a post-modern world.* Albany: State University of New York Press.

Orr, D. (2002). *The nature of design: Ecology, culture, and human intention.* New York: Oxford University Press.

O'Sullivan, E. (1999). *Transformative learning: Educational vision for the 21st century.* London: Zed Books.

Pack, J. R. (1991). The opportunities and constraints of privatization. In W. T. Gormley (Ed.), *Privatization and its alternatives* (pp. 281–306). Madison: University of Wisconsin Press.

Paire, J. R. (1998, November 6). What educators want to put in the schools of the future. *Atlanta Business Cronicle,* pp. 17–18.

Pelkki, J. A. (1994). The Saginaw River project. *Green Teacher, 37,* 32–33.

Perelman, L. J. (1992). *School's out: Hyperlearning, the new technology, and the end of education.* New York: William Morrow.

Perkins, L. (1957). *Work place for learning.* New York: Reinhold.

Perkins, L. B. (2001). *Building type basics for elementary and secondary schools*. New York: John Wiley & Sons.

Piaget, J. (1973). *The child and reality*. New York: Penguin Books.

Piestrup, A. M. (1984). A computer in the nursery school. In D. Peterson (Ed.), *Intelligent schoolhouse: Readings on computers and learning* (pp. 211–217). Reston, VA: Simon & Schuster.

Pike, G., & Selby, D. (1991). *Global teacher, global learner*. London: Trafalgar.

Polakow, V. (1992). *The erosion of childhood* (2nd ed.). Chicago: University of Chicago Press.

Poole, R. (1985). The politics of privatization. In S. M. Butler (Ed.), *The privatization options: A strategy to shrink the size of government.* (pp. 33–50). Washington, DC: The Heritage Foundation.

Presler, F. (1992). A letter to the architects. In E. Hebert & A. Meek (Eds.), *Children, learning, and school design* (pp. 59–63). Winnetka, IL: Winnetka Public Schools.

Qvortrup, L. (2002). Cyberspace as representation of space experience: In defense of a phenomenological approach. In L. Qvortrup (Ed.), *Virtual space: Spatiality in virtual inhabited 3D worlds*. London: Springer.

Reading, J., & Taven, G. (1996). Outdoor classrooms: The learning links. *Green Teacher, 47,* 29–31.

Relph, E. (1976). *Place and placelessness*. London: Pion.

Rieselbach, A. (1990). Building and learning. *Teachers College Record, 92*(2), 272–285.

Robertson, H. (1998). *No more teachers, no more books: The commercialization of Canada's schools*. Toronto: McClelland & Stewart.

Sack, R. D. (1980). *Conceptions of space in social thought: A geographic perspective*. Minneapolis: University of Minnesota Press.

Sanoff, H. (1994). *School design*. New York: Van Nostrand Reinhold.

Savage, T. V., & Armstrong, D. G. (2004). *Effective teaching in elementary social studies*. (5th Ed.). Columbus, OH: Pearson.

Schools mull buying terrorism insurance. (2003, January 24). *The Associated Press,* p. 3.

Sharp, D. (1966). *Modern architecture and expressionism*. London: Longman.

Sharp, R., & Green, A. (1975). *Education and social control: A study in progressive primary education*. London: Routledge.

Shepard, P. (1977). Place and human development. In *Children, nature, and the urban environment: Proceedings of a symposium-fair* (pp. 7–12). Washington, DC: U.S. Government Printing House.

Shields, C. M. (2000). *Year-round schooling: Promises and pitfalls*. Lanham, MD: Scarecrow Press.

Sime, J. D. (1995). Creating places or designing spaces? In L. Groat (Ed.), *Giving places meaning* (p. 23–41). London: Academic Press.

Smith, S. (2001). *The democratic potential of charter schools*. New York: Peter Lang.

Sobel, D. (1993). *Children's special places: Exploring the role of forts, dens, and bush houses in middle childhood*. Tucson, AZ: Zephyr Press.

Sobel, D. (1998). *Mapmaking with children: Sense of place education for the elementary years*. New York: Heinemann.

Spiller, N. (1998). *Digital dreams: Architecture and the new alchemic technologies*. London: Ellipsis.

Spodek, B. (1975). Open education: Romance or liberation? In B. Spodek & H. J. Walberg (Eds.), *Studies in open education* (pp. 212–229). New York: Agathon Press.

Spring, J. (1998). *Education and the global economy*. Mahwah, NJ: Lawrence Erlbaum Associates.

Standing, E. M. (1984). *Maria Montessori: Her life and work*. New York: Penguin Books.

Steiner, R. (1982). *The roots of education*. London: Rudolf Steiner Press.

Stennett, R. G., & Earl, L. M. (1983). Students' achievement, behavior, and physiology. *Alberta Education*, 67–77.

Sutton, S. E. (1996). *Weaving a tapestry of resistance: The places, power, and poetry of a sustainable society*. Westport, CT: Bergin & Garvey.

Tapscott, D. (1998). *Growing up digital: The rise of the net generation*. New York: McGraw-Hill.

Theobald, P. (1997). *Teaching the commons: Place, pride and the renewal of community*. Boulder, CO: Westview Press.

Titman, W. (1994). *Special place, special people: The hidden curriculum of school grounds*. Godalming, UK: World Wide Fund for Nature (UK).

Toronto Star. (1998, August 15). Back to the classroom—a mouldy portable. *Toronto Star*, p. 23.

Tuan, Y. (1977). *Space and place: The perspective of experience*. Minneapolis: University of Minnesota Press.

Tye, K. A. (1999). *Global education: A world wide movement*. Orange, CA: Independence Press.

U.S. Department of Education. (1996). *Getting America's students ready for the 21st Century: Meeting the technology literacy challenge*. Washington, DC.: Author.

U.S. Department of Education. (1997). *School construction and technology: Preparing our schools for the Information Era*. Washington, DC: Author.

U.S. Department of Education. (2001). *Statistical data for U.S. schools, 1999–2000*. Washington, DC: Author.

U.S. Environmental Protection Agency. (1996). *Indoor air quality basics for schools*. Washington, DC: Author.

U.S. General Accounting Office. (1997). *Summary of findings of recent studies on the school infrastructure problem*. Washington, DC: U.S. Department of Education.

U.S. General Accounting Office. (1999). *Pesticides: Use, effects, and alternatives to pesticides in schools*. Washington, DC: U.S. Department of Education.

Van Matre, S. (1974). *Acclimatizing: A personal and reflective approach to a natural relationship*. Martinsville, IN: American Camping Association.

Vecchi, V. (1998). What kind of space for living well in school? In G. Ceppi and M. Zini (Eds.), *Children, spaces, relations: Metaproject for an environment for young children* (pp. 128–135). Rome, Italy: Reggio Children.

Walker, L. (1992). School design in the 1990s: Outlook and prospects. In E. Hebert & A. Meek (Eds.), *Children, learning, and school design* (pp. 7–17). Winnetka, IL: Winnetka Public Schools.

Wiegand, P. (1992). *Places in the primary school: Knowledge and understanding of places at key stages 1 and 2*. London: Falmer Press.

Winston, B. (1998). *Media technology and society: A history from the telegraph to the Internet*. London: Routledge.

Wise, H. A. (1939). *Motion pictures as an aid in teaching American history*. New Haven, CT: Yale University Press.

Woelfel, N., & Tyler, K. (1945). *Radio and the school*. Yonkers, NY: Work Book Co.

INDEX

ABOUT THE AUTHOR

David Hutchison, Ph.D., is an Associate Professor in the Faculty of Education, Brock University (Ontario, Canada), and the author of *Growing Up Green: Education for Ecological Renewal* (Teachers College Press, 1998).